FROM CITY TO COUNTRYSIDE

A Guidebook to the Landmarks
of Augusta, Georgia

By: Bryan M. Haltermann

Published with the cooperation of Historic Augusta, Inc.

Library of Congress Catalog Card Number 96-080508

ISBN Number: 0-9650988-4-8 Hardcover
                       0-9650988-2-6 Softcover

All photographs by Bryan M. Haltermann except historic photographs in historical context section which are in the private collection of Bryan M. Haltermann, except for the photo facing the title page, which was provided by Drake White, Augusta, Georgia.

Book design by Cynthia L. Watke of Watke Creative Advertising of Augusta, Georgia, and Chris Howerdd of Phorum, Augusta Georgia. Printed by Bookcrafters, Fredericksburg, Virginia.

Contents

Preface

Long and winding, the Savannah River flows from the foot hills and creek beds of upper South Carolina and Georgia to the Atlantic Ocean. Below its rocky headwaters, where the rolling piedmont and sandy coastal plain meet, lies Augusta, Georgia.

At first glance, Augusta looks like any other American city established during the eighteenth and nineteenth centuries. Successive layers of suburban development separate the historic city center from a vast, rural countryside. Main traffic arteries such as Washington Road and the Gordon Highway connect a downtown district built mainly during the nineteenth century with suburban centers built after World War II. Moving from Broad Street to the most recently built suburbs in Richmond, Columbia, and Aiken Counties, there is a gradual shift from an urban landscape of buildings and pavement to a natural landscape of suburban yards, woodlands and farms.

Within the framework of these general development patterns, however, Augusta's appearance is unique. The source of this character is, in part, the shape and texture of local building history. By American standards, Augusta is an old city with a variety of neighborhoods and a spectrum of building design. From farmhouses to skyscrapers and from suburban dwellings to factories, Augusta has examples of nearly every architectural style popular on the eastern seaboard over the last 200 years.

Although it was established in 1736 on the southern edge of the British colonial frontier, it was during the nineteenth and early-twentieth centuries that many buildings and neighborhoods were created. Often, these historic structures are present-day Augusta's most widely recognized landmarks. The special buildings, districts, and landscapes which give Augusta its unique appearance and character are the subject of this book.

The twin goals of this book are to identify local landmarks as examples of architectural style or type, and to interpret the development of Augusta's built environment, the total picture of buildings, streets, and neighborhoods, through its historical development. The following photographs and text are meant to suggest a way of looking at Augusta by focusing on the details and context of local architecture. By identifying landmarks, both familiar and obscure, this book should help answer the question: how has Augusta grown?

A guide to local architecture can be useful beyond merely acting as an historical record. Recognizing landmarks, especially in relation to the ongoing process of development, is one of the first steps in forging a public plan to preserve them. Understanding established relationships among buildings, streets, and neighborhoods is fundamental to either renovating existing buildings or designing new ones which complement rather than compete with their surroundings.

The buildings and sites in this book are grouped according to three broad geographical sections: city, suburbs, and countryside. The economic history and values of these three areas differ and have resulted in varying neighborhood density and design. Commercial Broad Street, with its nearly solid wall of masonry facades flanking an exceptionally wide street, for instance, has a completely different architecture than suburban Walton Way or rural Richmond County.

Within the following geographical sections, buildings are arranged in chronological order. Building dates, however, should be used with this qualification: before the twentieth century, construction tended to be a slow process. Except for the simplest structures, ground breaking and completion of a house, not to mention a factory, hotel, or skyscraper, rarely occurred in a single year.

Some post-World War II buildings are included here as landmarks. Although many skyscrapers and industrial complexes, for instance, do not fit the widely accepted definition of historic (a structure built over fifty years ago with irreplaceable building design, craftsmanship, or materials), some are important for their unique design or as symbols of recent trends in construction and development.

Although this guidebook focuses on historic buildings, it is not meant to be a complete survey of local historic resources. There are not enough pages here, or in five books this size, to include every building which contributes to Augusta's character. Summerville, for instance, is the area's largest historic district containing approximately 770 acres and over 2,000 buildings. Augusta's suburban architecture, especially examples from the first three decades of the twentieth century, is especially varied and probably deserves a study of its own.

Instead of complete coverage, the following photographs are meant to represent prominent types, styles, and trends, and act as a field guide for exploring Augusta. Although it has not been a goal of this guidebook to show demolished buildings, some are included because they were standing when this project began in 1988.

It would be hard to overestimate the effect of a southern climate and the local economy on Augusta's architecture. Before the widespread use of air-conditioning after World War II, for instance, local buildings were designed for the warm, humid climate of eastern Georgia. Surrounded by a vast agricultural region and remote from Atlantic coast ports, nineteenth-century Augusta housewrights created buildings combining functional solutions to the southern climate and conservative versions of national styles. Although twentieth century building tends to display a mass-produced regularity, a blend of national and regional design still characterizes many newly built areas of Augusta.

Finally, within the context of local building, the natural landscape of open space, tree-lined streets, and private yards is an essential dimension of local landmarks. On both private and public land, there has often been a substantial effort to take advantage of the mild, southern climate by planting a lush landscape. The springtime bloom of azaleas, magnolias, and dogwoods is an unforgettable part of Augusta.

Many people have lent friendly support to the production of this book. The first acknowledgment is to Historic Augusta, Inc., which has provided encouragement for this project. Also, Erick Montgomery, Executive Director of Historic Augusta, H. M. Osteen, Jr., original Chairman of the project committee, Patrick G. Blanchard, Current Executive Board Member of Historic Augusta and W. Penland Mayson, Jr., President of Historic Augusta when the project was adopted, deserve many thanks.

John Linley of Athens, Georgia, and William R. Mitchell, Jr., of Atlanta both read early versions of this manuscript and lent their expertise in the field of Georgia architectural history. Edward Rice made helpful comments on the appearance of this book. Cynthia Watke of Watke Creative Advertising spent long hours and late nights designing and producing this book.

To all these people, I am very grateful.

Bryan M. Haltermann
January, 1997

House on 500 block Walton Way

HISTORICAL CONTEXT

The Eighteenth Century

Below the headwaters of the Savannah River, colonial authorities established two fortified trading posts during the eighteenth century. The first was Fort Moore, which was erected in 1716 downstream from present-day Augusta on the South Carolina shore. In 1736, three years after founding Georgia and its principal city Savannah, colonial trustee James Edward Oglethorpe issued orders for a surveyor and a company of soldiers to locate Fort Augusta. Only 127 miles from Savannah measured in a direct line, but over 200 miles along the winding river, Augusta was laid out on a level plain just down stream from the Savannah's fall line shoals. Describing the site in 1773, Philadelphia naturalist William Bartram wrote:

> Augusta, thus seated at the head of navigation, and just below the conflux of several of its most considerable branches, is without a competitor and commands the trade and commerce of vast fruitful regions above it; and I do not hesitate to pronounce, as my opinion, that it will soon become the metropolis of Georgia.

Like Bartram, Georgia's eighteenth century leaders saw Augusta as a principal town which was planned for easy expansion. Georgia's founder General Oglethorpe was part of a generation of English reformers concerned with urban congestion. In theory, Georgia's early colonial towns were laid out to avoid the overcrowded, impoverished districts and haphazard street plans of many European cities. To accomplish this, Oglethorpe, the colonial trustees, and their agents used modified street grids to create colonial towns like Savannah, Frederica, and Augusta.

For Augusta, General Oglethorpe ordered a grid plan of wide streets that provided for open squares, which were probably located within the original 300-foot width of Board Street. A 1780 map extending an existing grid pattern suggests that Augusta's street plan - the city's most enduring design - dates from the colonial period.
At least on paper, colonial Augusta was a well-planned town. Forty

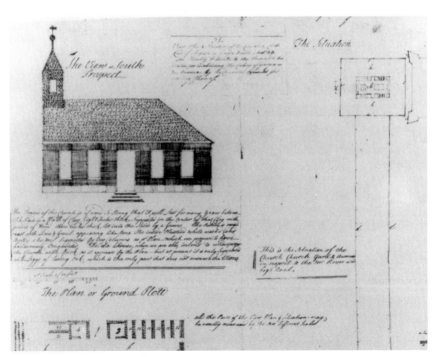

Plan of St. Paul's Church, about 1750.

one-acre lots were laid out with Broad Street and Fifth (Center) Street designed as the main, cross streets. The river, the street grid, Fort Augusta, and St. Paul's Church were colonial Augusta's land marks. During the eighteenth century and the first half of the nineteenth century, local builders used traditional techniques, designs, and a limited number of indigenous materials. The result was a local building vernacular characterized by frontier simplicity rather than urban high style.

Throughout the colonial era, the haphazard location of buildings on Augusta's town lots rarely reinforced the appearance of a regular grid plan. The geometry of the plan was not always evident to either citizens or visitors. Beyond the intended order of the eighteenth-century town, Broad and Fifth (Center) Streets became meandering rural roads. By following existing topography, these rough thoroughfares typically changed direction to avoid natural obstacles. In the rolling piedmont above Augusta, many of the earliest roads followed the high ground along ridges. The area's earliest rural roads led from Augusta's street grid to the nearby towns such as Savannah, Wrightsboro, Milledgeville, and Washington-Wilkes. Today, these major roads lead from the city and direct suburban development.

Following the final evacuation of British troops from Georgia at the end of the American Revolution in 1783, Augusta became the gate way for settlers traveling to the vast, unsettled pineland of piedmont Georgia. Pioneers typically reached Augusta from two routes: up the Savannah River from the Atlantic coast or down the backcountry valleys of the Carolinas, Virginia, and Pennsylvania.

Newcomers often brought the traditional building practices which characterized the rural communities from which they came. Local builders then modified these conservative designs to suit Augusta's climate. As a result, the appearance of Augusta before 1850 was casual and provincial. A plan for Saint Paul's Church in 1750, for instance, outlined a medieval building system of post and beam framing filled with a plasterlike mixture of lime and sand. Most local buildings, however, were built from the most plentiful indigenous material, southern yellow pines. Different woods were used for special purposes, like cypress for roof shingling, while brick, fieldstone, and quarried granite were used for foundations and chimneys. Except for public or exceptional private buildings, eighteenth-century architecture in Augusta typically emphasized functional requirements over formal style. During the increasingly rapid settlement of the southern backcountry during the late 19th century, Augusta was the last town on the way to the frontier which, at least in theory, had been laid out by London-based colonial trustees.

During the American Revolution, a 1780 Legislative Act law established a new local government for Augusta and extended the grid beyond its colonial limits. The act provided for the division and sale of a strip of the Town Common south of Greene Street, required new lot owners to build houses of minimum dimensions under penalty of foreclosure, and prevented anyone from buying more than one new lot. Larger lots were reserved from the Town Common for a public cemetery, an academy, a city hall, a jail, and churches. In this era of rampant speculation in newly-opened rural land, the legislature prescribed an orderly and regular expansion for Georgia's fastest-growing town.

Guided by the founding town plan, but undoubtedly influenced by the Congressional adoption of the grid as the basis for the National Survey in 1785, the Augusta City Council regularly extended the grid throughout the Town Common. Following demand for new sites, rows or "ranges" of new lots were laid out on the southern edge of the town simply by adding east-west streets.

Walker Street, for instance, was laid out in 1809. North-south streets were simply extended. Because of Augusta's level site, this pattern was generally adhered to until private developers laid out winding streets in the 1920s for pioneering automobile suburbs such as Forrest Hills.

Although Augusta was the first state capital from 1785 to 1794, no major building survives from this period. Augusta's earliest existing buildings date from the 1790s and were built on rural sites surrounding the town.

Early Nineteenth Century Expansion

During the nineteenth century, when many Augusta leaders supported the national Whig platform of internal improvements for economic expansion, city government was especially active in deciding what the river town should look like. By laying out an orderly street plan, constructing civic buildings such as wharves, public markets, and firehouses, and sponsoring other projects aimed at the expansion of trade and industry, local government played an important role in shaping Augusta's appearance.

As the town grew from a frontier outpost to a commercial center, then to an industrial city beginning in the 1840s, Augusta was transformed from a village to a city of specialized commercial, residential, and industrial neighborhoods. Many of these - such as Broad Street,

Greene Street, "Pinch Gut" (Olde Towne), Laney-Walker, the Augusta Canal, and Harrisburg - are historic districts today.

During the nineteenth century, cotton trading was Augusta's leading commercial activity. The transportation, sale, and milling of cotton fueled the local economy and was the impetus for a significant amount of local building. As the nearest inland port and market town for a large agricultural hinterland in both Georgia and South Carolina, Augusta's economy relied heavily on cotton and its transportation to both local and national markets.

After the invention of the cotton gin in 1794 made large-scale cotton farming widespread, Augusta's role as a cotton center was spurred by three events: the introduction of steamboats on the Savannah River in 1817, the arrival of the railroads in the 1840s, and the construction of cotton factories along the Augusta Canal beginning in the late 1840s. The river, the canal, the railroads, and the surrounding agricultural countryside made Augusta, first and foremost, a cotton town.

For Augusta cotton factors and other merchants, high market prices generally meant a strong economy. This led to the construction of Broad Street stores, Reynolds Street warehouses, elaborate cotton factories along the Augusta Canal, townhouses throughout the city, and summer houses on nearby ridges. Private buildings with major public buildings like the courthouse, the city market, and the churches, created the appearance of Augusta before the twentieth century.

Certain local streets were also nineteenth century landmarks. Broad Street, for instance, has been Augusta's most prominent street, both in appearance and use. Its width was reduced from 300 to 166 feet in the 1790s, but its position as the major downtown avenue has never changed. Tyrone Powers, an Irishman visiting Augusta in 1842, described Broad Street like this:

Public market building in the center of Broad Street east of Fifth (Center St.)

Augusta consists of one very wide street, a couple of miles in length, and is composed of a mixed description of buildings; many of the houses and stores being

of wood, and exceedingly humble in appearance;
others are built of brick, large, handsome, and well
fitted up in emulation of those in the northern cities.

Lined with crepe myrtles from 1801 until a large fire destroyed them
in 1829, Broad Street acted as a firebreak, an open space for air circulation, and, in many respects, the town center. The width of
Augusta's main avenue reflects the nineteenth-century belief that air
circulation afforded by wide streets was an antidote to the miasma of
stagnant air and disease. Recurring fever epidemics, like the 1839
outbreak of yellow fever which struck nearly one third of the city
population, depressed the local economy by discouraging farmers
from coming to town for business. A public market in the center of
the street below Fifth (Center) and the Upper Market below Twelfth
(Marbury) Street were public buildings important for both their
functional and their visual roles. They marked the edges of Broad
Street's commercial development and, by blocking the vista up the
wide avenue, created an enclosed plaza with a planned, urban quality.

The width of downtown streets matched the generally large scale of
individual building design. To promote coolness and air circulation,
interior rooms before the advent of air conditioning had high ceil-
ings, large windows, and, often, wide hallways. Balconies, especially
on Broad Street commercial townhouses, were common, while
porches were standard for residential buildings.

As Tyrone Powers observed, stores and residences were typically built
side by side on Broad Street. By necessity, people lived near their
places of work. The most obvious 19th century example is Augusta
merchants living above their Broad Street stores. Beginning in the

second quarter of the century, however, prosperous merchants moved from their Broad Street commercial townhouses to detached dwellings on the fringes of the commercial district. Early nineteenth century city leaders (like Nicholas Ware and John Phinizy) usually lived near the city center.

Colonial officials and, later, the Augusta City Council planned other major avenues parallel to the river. Second in size and importance only to Broad, Greene Street developed after 1820 as one of the city's most prominent residential streets. Unlike the commercial town houses set directly on Broad Street, detached residences with shallow front yards typically were built along Greene Street. By the 1830s, the city had established a tree-lined park in the street median. "The Greene" or "The Grove", as it was called, was a planned promenade a popular feature of nearly every major nineteenth-century European city - which became the location for a series of commemorative monuments. The fifty-foot high Signers Monument, for instance, was

City Hall, 1819

built about 1850. The construction of the city hall and courthouse (1820) and a number of prominent churches including First Baptist (1819,1903), Saint John Methodist (1844), Second

Presbyterian (Union Baptist, 1851), Saint James Methodist (1856, 1886), First Christian (1876), Greene Street Presbyterian (1906) and sacred heart (1898) gave Greene Street a monumental, public quality which, in some ways, rivaled commercial Broad Street.

While the wide avenues parallel to the river - Reynolds, Broad, Greene, and Telfair - are the city's most prominent streets, the system of regular cross streets completes Augusta's grid system. During the eighteenth century, Fifth (Center) was the most prominent, leading from a ferry crossing at the river to the City Market located in the center of Broad. The ferry was replaced by a toll bridge in 1795. The market was an open, arcade building which, from 1830 until its destruction by an 1878 cyclone, had a neoclassical portico, clock tower, and cupola.

Parallel to Fifth (Center), regular north-south cross streets run from the Savannah River south to the city limits. Originally named for local, state, and national leaders, these cross streets were renamed First through Fifteenth in the 1880s. Approximately sixty-six feet wide, the cross streets are nearly identical in size and in character except for Fifth (Center) and Thirteenth (McKinne). From the nineteenth century to the present, these two cross streets have marked Broad Street commercial development and led to bridges over the Savannah River.

By the 1850s, the grid plan had spread to natural limits. East Boundary and South Boundary (later renamed Gwinnett Street, then Laney-Walker Boulevard) were bounded by swamps, and West Boundary (later renamed Carnes Road, then Fifteenth Street) was bounded by Hawk's Gulley. Throughout the antebellum period, the boundary streets generally marked the edge of development, creating a clear division between town and surrounding countryside. Later in the century, however, this division became less clear. Vacant land was developed between Augusta and neighboring rural villages such as Harrisonville, Summerville, and Harrisburg.

Victorian Era Augusta And The Arrival Of Railroads
The Canal And Factories

While the framework for nineteenth century Augusta building typically followed the straight lines of the local grid plan, new industrial projects built during the 1850s introduced a different pattern. An early industrial enterprise was the construction of the Georgia Railroad beginning in 1836. The railroad line was built through the southwest quadrant of the city, curving gradually to a depot near the corner of Walker and Eighth (Jackson) Streets. The railroad created a new street, Railroad Street, (renamed University Place, now R.A. Dent Boulevard) whose path ran diagonally to the dominant street grid. At the end of the railroad line, the company built a roundhouse and repair yard which anchored Augusta's first industrial neighborhood between Walker and Fenwick Streets.

This industrial corridor divided the city into two districts. To the north was the waterfront, commercial main street, public buildings, and the city's most prominent residential neighborhoods. To the south a new, less affluent residential district grew along an extension of the established grid street plan.

Other railroads followed the Georgia Railroad into Augusta. In the mid 1850s, the Augusta and Waynesboro Railroad (later a branch of the Central of Georgia Railroad, the Georgia Railroad's main rival for piedmont trade), built a depot in open land south of Fenwick Street at Sixth (Washington) Street. In 1857, after a fourteen-year prohibition against crossing the Savannah River, the City Council allowed the South Carolina Railroad, the pioneering line which connected Charleston to Augusta's cross-river rival Hamburg in 1833, to cross the river and build a depot on Reynolds Street west of Fifth (Center) Street. In 1882, the Charleston and Western Carolina Railroad built tracks along the river front, roughly paralleling the course of the upper canal past the Sibley and King mills.

Besides bringing tracks into the heart of the city, the railroads linked Augusta with other parts of the Southeast. The railroads contributed to a decade of local economic prosperity and an unprecedented building boom. As additional railroad lines created a nationwide network after the Civil War, railroads brought Augusta closer to an economic and cultural mainstream. This trend from regional to national transportation systems coincided with more uniform building design in Augusta.

During the 1840s and 1850s, technological advances also influenced local building practices. Steam-powered cutting, planing, and molding machines, like those at William H. Goodrich's factory on Reynolds Street or at Quien and Rigby's factory near Thirteenth (McKinne) Street, produced more uniform framing and decorative building components. Georgia foundries began producing cast iron building parts, especially balconies and columns, in the late 1840s. Steam-powered printing presses turned out widely-circulated pattern books which promoted national over vernacular design. In Augusta, a combination of new technology and generally high cotton prices during the 1850s meant a high volume of new buildings in the nationally popular Greek Revival and Italianate styles.

Besides public buildings, the City of Augusta participated in other development projects. After a local economic downturn from 1840 to 1845, a company headed by local businessmen began the construction of the Augusta Canal as a source of power and as a route to transport goods past the river shoals into the city. Public support was pivotal for financing the unprecedented construction project, which was completed in 1846. The City Council issued bonds to raise capital and, after cost overruns, purchased the canal company stock and became its owner and operator. By 1850, private investors had built several textile, machine, and grain mills, making the $10 million investment in Augusta industry the largest in any Georgia city.

By the mid-nineteenth century, Augusta's development followed a predictable pattern. Generally, the commercial district extended from the working waterfront to Broad Street. This area was dominated by brick warehouses and commercial townhouses. Detached residences, both frame and brick, were built on all sides of the commercial district. Industry and its related housing were built on the southern and western fringes of the city.

During the Civil War from 1861 to 1865, the Confederate Government fueled the local economy with new building projects. The new government commissioned the construction of ordinance factories at the former United States Arsenal in Summerville and a large gunpowder complex a quarter of a mile west of the city limits on the banks of the canal (C. Shaler Smith, 1862). The thirteen building Confederate Powder Works was one of the largest in the world. Its brick design featured the crenelated towers and parapets reminiscent of sixteenth-century English fortresses. Although these buildings were later dismantled, Augusta was one of the few major Confederate cities never occupied by Union troops during the war. Without military destruction, the local economy was poised for new, postwar expansion.

In 1872, the City of Augusta began the enlargement of the Augusta Canal. Over the next decade, a series of new factories was built in the western edge of the city and in Harrisburg. The construction of the King Mill and the Sibley Manufacturing Company on the former site of the Confederate Powder Works, for example, prompted the construction of row houses, apartment buildings, and small frame residences for mill workers. When Harrisburg was annexed to the city in

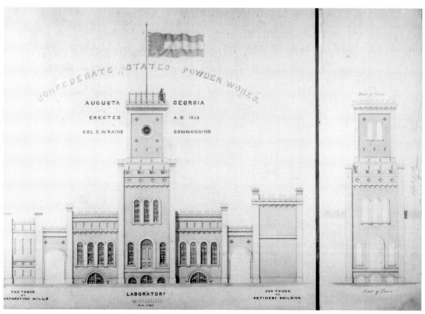

Plan of Confederate States Powder Works, 1864; By Capt. C. Shaler Smith

1883, it was in the process of transformation from a rural village to a suburb of cottages on narrow town lots.

About the same time, a similar neighborhood was developing on the southern edge of the city. Originally home to workers in the nearby railway yards and factories, Laney-Walker is bounded on the east by Sixth (Washington) Street and on the west by Thirteenth (McKinne) Street. Railroad lines run along both streets. The area of generally simple, single-story frame houses became the home of Augusta's black community by the last quarter of the nineteenth century. During an economic boom from 1912 to 1929, commercial buildings for black owned businesses, such as the Penny Savings Bank (1922), made Laney-Walker Boulevard more commercial and less residential in character.

After the national depression from 1873 to 1878, the local economy began to benefit from the enlargement of the Augusta Canal (1872 1875). New cotton factories, such as the Empire, the King, and the Sibley, and new railroad lines helped make Augusta one of the largest inland cotton markets in the United States. In 1886, Augusta's cotton brokers and factors built an exchange building on the corner of Reynolds and Eighth (Jackson). This building served as the head quarters for the business which had dominated the working river front and its adjacent warehouses for over seventy years. The cotton business remained a cornerstone of the local economy until the arrival of the boll weevil in Georgia about 1918 and the failure of Barrett and Company, one of Augusta's largest cotton brokerages, in 1923.

Besides a surge in commercial and industrial construction during the late 1880s and 1890s, an increase in service jobs in Augusta meant the construction of new office buildings downtown. Practitioners of law, medicine, banking, real estate, and insurance increased rapidly and caused the construction of multi-story Broad Street buildings completely devoted to office use. A pioneering new example was the Dyer Building. Built in 1891 at the northwest corner of Broad and Eighth (Jackson), the building had five stories and an electric elevator. It was destroyed in Augusta's large fire of 1916.

Augusta Electric Light and Motor Company, a private business, first provided electricity to Broad Street in 1882, and ten years later extended electric service to the entire city. Powered by five turbines located on the Augusta Canal, the company also produced electricity to operate the Augusta and Summerville Railroad Company, the local electric streetcar system which began operation in June 1890. The streetcar line eventually consisted of twenty-five miles of track, forty-six cars, and an "inter-urban" line to Aiken, South Carolina. By making the commute from downtown to new residential developments convenient, the system catalyzed development in suburbs such as Monte Sano, North Augusta, Druid Park, and Turpin Hill. From 1890 to 1901, for instance, Summerville's population increased nearly 400 percent.

The streetcar system helped make Augusta, in turn-of-the-century terms, a modern city with multiple layers of new suburban development.

Suburban Expansion

Although a number of rural and suburban villages were located around Augusta during the nineteenth century, Summerville is the

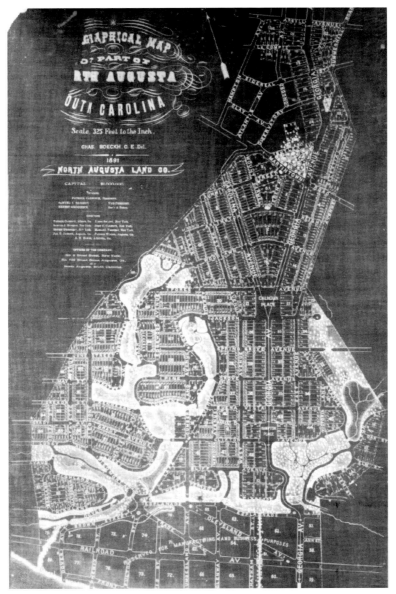

Plan of North Augusta, 1891

largest and best known. Established in the late 1790s as a small summer retreat on a ridge three miles west of downtown, it had a semirural character until the early 1890s. Although it had its own branch of Richmond Academy and its own cemetery, only thirty-five full time residents were listed in an 1865 Augusta directory.

Pre-1890 architecture tended to be simple and characterized by wood construction. Before the arrival of early Victorian-era pattern books about 1850, story-and-a-halfhouses known as Sand Hills cottages and two-story dwellings resembling farmhouses were built on lots usually ranging in size from two to ten acres.

The standard design for a Sand Hills cottage is a story-and-a-half frame building built over a finished, brick basement. Dormer windows (nearly identical to those on Broad Street commercial town houses) decorate a gable roof which often incorporates front and rear porches. Variations of these cottages were built in many southern port cities.

Summerville, sometimes called the Sand Hills or The Hill, developed along a simple grid street plan centered at Walton Way and Milledge Road. An area enclosed by a circle with a one-mile radius was incorporated by the state legislature in 1861 and annexed to the City of Augusta in 1912.

Increasingly accessible to downtown Augusta by plank road after 1850, a mule-drawn trolley after 1866, and an electric streetcar system after 1890 (all following the present route of Walton Way from Fifteenth Street west), the village grew as a modern, all-season suburb which increasingly competed with downtown for residents.

During the 1890s, suburban development in Summerville was coupled with the growth of a winter resort business. Between 1890 and 1933, three major resort hotels, polo fields, golf courses, and winter homes were built in Summerville. Along Milledge Road, the village's main north-south street, winter residents from northeastern and midwestern cities commissioned professional architects, especially the local Kemp and Wendell firm, to design rambling suburban houses. These winter homes resembled residences found in expensive suburbs located on the fringes of other U.S. cities.

The Twentieth Century City

Early in the twentieth century, a surge in commercial construction occurred which significantly altered the appearance

Sand Hills Cottage, Battle Row. H.A.B.S. photo.

of Broad Street. Before 1910, for instance, church spires, factory towers, and the cast iron fire tower known as "Big Steve" at Eighth (Jackson) and Greene (1860, dismantled 1895, 93.5 feet tall) were the city's tallest structures. The steeple of the First Christian Church (1876) at the corner of Seventh (McIntosh) and Greene, for instance, made it the tallest building in downtown Augusta before the twentieth century.

After the Otis Elevator Company introduced the first electric elevator in 1889 and steel-frame construction became common after 1890, new building height was possible. The pioneering examples of local skyscraper construction, the ten-story Marion Building and the sixteen-story Lamar Building, were both begun by 1913. Their silhou-

Eighth (Jackson) Street, Early 20th Century

ettes drastically changed Broad Street's appearance. Although they were gutted during the large downtown fire of 1916, both were rebuilt.

The exterior of both skyscrapers relied heavily on the use of terra-cotta. The baked clay components were used to create elaborate Broad Street facades and to fireproof the structural steel skeletons. During the 1890s, terra cotta was first used as an isolated detail on a number of Broad Street facades. But after 1900, large amounts of the material, cast in an endless variety of patterns, decorated commercial, residential and public buildings around the city.

Paralleling national building patterns, new residential development occurred in the suburbs while the character of downtown growth became increasingly commercial. The mixed-use character of nine-teenth century Broad Street was gradually replaced by a specialized commercial, entertainment, and office district. Repeated flooding of the Savannah River, the consequent construction of the levee begin-ning in 1913, and the extensive downtown fire of 1916 which burned thirty-two densely developed blocks also reinforced the resi-dential exodus from downtown.

The design of new downtown banks, movie theatres, apartment buildings, and stores increasingly followed national trends interpreted by a new group of local professional architects. G. Lloyd Preacher, Henry T. E. Wendell, Willis Irvin, and Lynn Drummond were part of the first generation of local architects who studied at architectural programs at Clemson, Cornell, and Georgia Tech. The use of archi-tects from larger cities was reserved for only a small group of major buildings like the Union Station (1902, Francis P. Milburn of

Columbia, SC), the U.S. Post Office (1914, Oscar Wenderoth of Washington, D.C.), and the Lamar Building (1913, William L. Stoddard of New York).

The twin impulse of reform politics and renewed interest in public architecture and landscaping led to local expressions of the national "City Beautiful" movement. A prominent example is the develop ment of the large lot north of Augusta's Beaux Arts railroad terminal, Union Station, as a landscaped urban square in 1912. Named Barrett Plaza, the square was a carefully planned open space decorated with a central, cast iron fountain, palmetto trees, and a statue of Augusta's reform mayor, Patrick Walsh.

Union Station

Beyond the surrounding brick-paved streets, a new U. S. Post Office and the Plaza Hotel (1914, G. Lloyd Preacher, demolished 1991) were built. The hotel was built only after plans for a large, neoclassi-cal city hall were proposed and later scrapped by the city administra-tion. Between 1912 and World War II, when passenger traffic on the

22

railroads reached a peak, Barrett Plaza was the gateway to Augusta. Other "City Beautiful" projects were the landscaped medians along Henry Street, Central Avenue, and Park Avenue.

Post World War II Expansion

During the nineteenth century, reputations of cities like Augusta usually rested on visitors' perceptions of government and commercial buildings. But during the twentieth century, residential suburbs, factories, shopping malls, and sporting venues increasingly defined a city's image. An Augusta example is the Masters golf tournament, giving the city an international reputation as a golf capital.

After World War II, an unprecedented building boom took place. Large industrial complexes and additional layers of residential sub-urbs were built beyond the city limits. During the early 1950s, Clarks Hill Dam, the Savannah River Plant, and Fort Gordon were all large, government-sponsored projects built on rural sites near Augusta. Each boosted the local economy with construction and permanent jobs. The largest example is the Savannah River Plant, which required over 50,000 acres of South Carolina farmlands, woodland, and former town sites for its nuclear reactor reservation.

During the 1960s, national corporations such as Procter and Gamble (1962), Continental Can (1960, now International Paper), and Columbia Nitrogen (1962, now Arcadian Corporation) built new factories in south Richmond County. New roads like the Gordon Highway (1950-1957), and enlarged versions of Washington Road and Walton Way provided easier access to new development in both southern and western Richmond County.

The design of new suburbs usually followed the precedent for curving street plans pioneered locally by Forrest Hills. Unlike the traditional street grid of the city and Summerville, street plans tend to reflect rolling topography. Forrest Hills was one of the last suburban neighborhoods annexed to the city in 1956. Since the 1950 census, city population steadily declined while suburban population increased dramatically.

New industrial jobs in the 1950s and 1960s meant residential development in the suburbs. In subdivisions like Country Club Hills (until 1942, the Lake Course of the Augusta Country Club), Murray Hill, National Hills, and Westwick, brick, single-story "ranch houses" and "split-levels" were built on lots whose informal landscapes easily blended together. Close to the suburbs and shoppers reliant on their cars, early shopping centers like Daniel Village (1958) on Wrightsboro Road provided convenient shopping.

Downtown, the seventeen-story Georgia Railroad Bank building (1968, now the First Union building), the ten-story Trust Company of Georgia building (1969, now the Sun Trust Building), and the twelve-story Executive House Hotel (1972, now the Landmark Hotel) redefined the Broad Street skyline. In contrast to the earlier Marion and the Lamar Buildings, the new towers featured low-relief, relatively austere designs executed in glass, metal, and masonry. By the 1970s, Augusta faced the same development trends common to other mid-sized American metropolitan areas. The city was divided into a commercial downtown surrounded by deteriorating residential neighborhoods built during the previous century. At the same time, layers of development further and further away from commercial Broad Street flourished with new suburbs, shopping centers, and low-rise office buildings.

After the construction of the initial local section of Interstate #20 in 1965, the strip commercial development along Washington Road began. Westward suburban expansion soon reached eastern Columbia County, and the Bobby Jones Expressway (1973, 1981), Augusta's version of a suburban perimeter road, connected two fast growing centers of metropolitan growth: Martinez (Columbia County) and South Augusta.

The concentration of new housing outside the city limits led to the opening of two regional malls in 1978. The Augusta Mall in West Augusta and the Regency Mall in South Augusta are focal points of suburban retail and entertainment activities. With vast parking lots and enclosed, climate-controlled shopping arcades, the malls quickly surpassed Broad Street's historic role as the city marketplace. In response, local government and business leaders followed the national

Riverwalk Park at Eighth (Jackson) Street

pattern of attempting to redevelop the economic vitality of Augusta's central business district.

During the mid 1970s, local leaders commissioned I.M. Pei and Partners to design two key projects. A New York architectural firm nationally known for its work on large-scale revitalization projects, the Pei firm planned the sunken parking areas and parks in the Broad Street median, The Chamber of Commerce building (1976), and the Augusta-Richmond County Coliseum (1979). This coliseum was built on the former site of the Georgia Railroad's roundhouse and repair yards near the intersection of Seventh (McIntosh) and Walker Streets.

Nearly a decade later, public redevelopment efforts turned to the river front. In 1988 the city-sponsored Riverwalk, a paved esplanade built on top of the levee (Cranston, Robertson and

Port Royal under construction, 1991.

Whitehurst, Engineers), was opened. Breeches in the river-front levee at Eighth (Jackson) and near Tenth (Cumming) Streets created an entrance to a linear river front park and amphitheater. Adjacent to the levee on sites formerly occupied by cotton warehouses, and a railroad line, two new buildings, Port Royal at Seventh (McIntosh) Street (1991, VGR Architects) and the Augusta Riverfront Center and the Radission Riverfront Hotel (1991, Smallwood, Reynolds, Stuart and Stuart) near Tenth (Cumming) Street, are downtown's newest multi-story buildings.

Like the local economic boom following the enlargement of the Augusta Canal in the 1870s, new development was actively promoted by city government during the late 1980s and 1990s. Instead of relying solely on the city's traditional role as a marketplace and transportation center, Augusta leaders have tried to breathe new life into the downtown area by marketing historic districts and the riverfront as tourist and convention centers. By encouraging development along the Savannah River and throughout downtown, city leaders are pursuing the kind of urban vision which was typical during the great city-building decades of the nineteenth and early twentieth centuries.

The City

I. The City

1. The Savannah River.

The Savannah River's approximately east-west course at Augusta has oriented the direction of local development for over 250 years. Located upstream from early development, the river's rocky shoals made Augusta the head of navigation and a natural commercial center for eastern Georgia and western South Carolina during the 18th and 19th centuries.

The South Carolina riverfront opposite Augusta was the site of the town of Hamburg from the early 1820s until the early 20th century. The town was located just west of the present-day Jefferson Davis Memorial Bridge (1931), (Fifth Street Bridge) and was the western terminus of the Charleston Railroad after 1833.

During the late 19th century, the Charleston and Western Carolina railroad (1882) and the Riverside Mill (1886) anchored a working waterfront of wharves and warehouses north of Reynolds Street. From 1913 to 1918, an approximately 18 foot-high earthen levee was built along the riverbank to prevent flooding. The levee obliterated a street, Bay Street, and blocked the view of the river from downtown.

Today, the Augusta Port Authority sponsors spring sporting events on the river including a rowing regatta and a powerboat race. New development linked by the Riverwalk esplanade, which opened in April 1988, has revived the river's role as a center of community life.

2. Broad Street Historic District.

Synonymous with downtown Augusta and the city's traditional main street commercial center, Broad Street has always been notable for its width and concentration of commercial buildings built in nearly every era from the late 18th century until the present. The widest of downtown Augusta's east-west avenues, Broad Street was the city's main public space during the 19th century.

Before World War I, commercial townhouses with ground-floor stores and residential apartments upstairs were typically built on narrow, deep lots from Fifth (Center) to Thirteenth (McKinne). Beyond these boundaries, Broad Street has a residential character of detached townhouses and a landscape median.

In 1829, an extensive fire caused City Council to create a fire district for the commercial section of Broad. Frame construction was forbidden, and masonry was required.

In the center of the street, the city government built market buildings just east of Fifth (Center) and, later just east of Twelfth (Marbury). These public buildings helped define a linear plaza for conducting 19th century trade. before the construction of early skyscrapers about 1913, hotels like the Planter's at Macartan Street, the Albion at present-day Albion Street, and the Arlington at Eighth (Jackson) Street were the largest buildings on Broad. From 1866 to 1937, a mule-drawn trolley, then an electric streetcar system, operated on tracks running down the center of the street.

The 78-foot Confederate Monument has marked the 700 block -

probably the block with the highest overall building density in the city - since its dedication in 1878.

Two and three-story buildings were replaced by buildings with up to five stories during the 1890's. A modern skyline was created about 1915 with the construction of the two steel-frame skyscrapers on the 700 block. Several fires during the 1890s and the extensive fire of 1916 destroyed many Broad Street buildings, especially east of 8th (Jackson) Street.

During the 1960s and 1970s, the towers of The Georgia Railroad Bank (now First Union bank), the Trust Company Bank (now SunTrust Bank) and the Executive House Hotel (now The Landmark Hotel) expanded the downtown skyline. In 1975, the Chamber of Commerce headquarters (I.M. and Partners) was built in the street median west of 6th (Jackson). The building has little of the visual impact of the 19th-century public markets. Part of a renovation plan of the mid-1970s was the construction of sunken, median parking (I.M. Pei and Partners) from the 500 block through the 900 block.

The Broad Street National Register Historic District was created in April, 1980 and runs from 5th (Center) to 13th (McKinne) and includes many of the small 19th-century buildings located just off Broad on the cross street. In the fall of 1988, the City of Augusta helped re-establish the 19th century appearance of the street by planting Chinese Elm trees along the sidewalk.

3. Louis C. Cantelou House.
366 Telfair Street (about 1810).

When it was built, this frame house was located on the eastern fringe of the city. Its frame construction, limited detailing, and simple interpretation of a two-story neoclassical portico would have been at home either in the country or town. Before the development of lower Telfair Street into narrow townhouse lots around 1850, this building stood alone on a city block in a semirural environment.

4. The First Presbyterian (Christ) Church,
640 Telfair Street (Robert Mills, 1812, 1848).

One of the oldest buildings in Augusta, the First Presbyterian Church was built on the southern edge of the city on one of the large Telfair Street lots reserved for early 19th century public buildings and churches.

Robert Mills, a South Carolina and a nationally prominent professional architect during the Federal era, designed Christ Church, as it was first called. Mid 19th century renovations, including Romanesque windows, front door, and crenelations, however, have replaced the original late neoclassical details, especially the fanlight window sash. The churchyard is a parklike lot of informal landscaping enclosed, in 19th century fashion, by a wooden fence matching the scale of the building.

5. St. Paul's Episcopal Church, *605 Reynolds Street,*
(Henry Wendell and R. H. Robertson of New York, 1919).

Due to its location near the river, Fort Augusta, and the western edge of 18th century settlement, St. Paul's Episcopal Church is a landmark of colonial Augusta. Surrounded by a brick wall with a cast- and wrought-iron entrance gate, the church graveyard was Augusta's public cemetery before the creation of Magnolia Cemetery in 1818. The tombstones are a record of the varied birthplaces and occupations of late 18th century Augusta citizens. The most elaborate are decorated with neoclassical urns.

Once the center of St. Paul's parish, the colonial unit of government, the church now occupies its fourth building. Local architect Henry Wendell, associated with New York architect R. H. Robertson, designed the existing building closely along the lines of the former church building (1820, John Lund), which burned in downtown Augusta's large 1916 fire.

The design is based on a combination of Georgian and Federal details, a standard Greek Revival temple front, and the crisp contrast between red brick walls and white trim. The front facade is a Parthenon-style Doric portico, which became a popular feature of many public buildings during the Greek Revival. A central bell tower capped with a neoclassical belfry penetrates the massive portico and remains a noticeable part of the downtown skyline.

41

6. Gertrude Herbert Memorial Institute of Art,
506 Telfair Street (1818).

This early 19th century townhouse is the most sophisticated example of residential Federal architecture in Augusta. Due to its high cost and its commission by Mayor Nicholas Ware, it became known as "Ware's Folly" after its completion.

The house is built above its brick basement in wood, the area's most abundant and commonly used building material during the 18th and 19th centuries. With matching, two-story bays flanking a bowed, two story portico, the Telfair Street facade is the heart of the design. Exterior and interior stairways, and fanlight over doors and central dormer window are based on the ellipse, the geometric motif commonly used in high-style Federal design.

In 1937, Mrs. John W. Herbert (Site #57, 2259 Cumming Road) bought the building to establish the Gertrude Herbert Memorial Institute of Art as a memorial to her daughter.

7. Greene Street Historic District.

As a downtown avenue, Greene Street has always been second in importance only to Broad Street. This residential street was planned as a boulevard with a landscaped median at the beginning of the 19th century. Along with the central "Greene Walk or "The Grove," detached townhouses with shallow front yards give the street a spacious, carefully planned character. This street was Augusta's version of the showcase residential streets planned on other U.S. cities in the early to mid 19th century.

Greene Street has been the traditional home of local government. The neoclassical Richmond County Courthouse (1820, 1892) was demolished after the construction of the Augusta-Richmond County Municipal Building in 1957, A High Victorian Romanesque brick and terra cotta United States Post Office (1890, later used as City Hall, 1915-1957) at the corner of Ninth (Campbell), was replaced by the Main Branch of the Augusta-Richmond County Library (Eve and Stulb, 1960).

Early 19th century buildings, like the Eve House at 619, tended to be simple, frame, and built directly on the public right of way. As a group, the mid and late 19th century townhouses on Greene, often built of brick, were the largest and most elaborate in Augusta.

The construction of commemorative monuments in the tree-lined median, beginning with the obelisk-style Signers (originally Hall and Walton) Monument about 1850, made Greene Street the model of a Beaux-Arts boulevard by the end of the 19th century.

The elevated Gordon Highway, 1953-1957, cuts Greene Street between Fourth (Elbert) and Fifth (Center), making a barrier between the "Pinched Gut" Historic District to the east and the Greene Street Historic District on the west. The connection of the elevated John C. Calhoun Expressway to upper Greene Street in 1985, a road which ties the post-World-War-II commercial strip on Washington Road to the 19th century city, makes the street less of a destination and more of a thoroughfare to other places downtown.

The median, however, remains an unmistakable landmark and was the basis for Greene Street's listing on the National Register in 1980.

8. 608 Broad Street *(about 1843)*.

Before the 1830s, local commercial buildings often looked like over-grown residences. This example was built, or possibly rebuilt, as a commercial townhouse sometime after the 1829 Broad Street fire. The two-and-a-half-story design with dormer windows was typical of all types of early 19th century Broad Street buildings. The cast-iron balcony and columns must have been installed after the late 1840s when foundries began manufacturing cast iron building components.

A central door and stairway originally divided the two first-story commercial bays and led upstairs to a spacious story-and-a-half apart-ment. Similar to 601 Broad located on the opposite side of the street, this rather horizontal building is a reminder of the low-density appearance of Augusta before the arrival of industry in the 1840's.

The building was renovated after Historic Augusta's Revolving Fund bought and resold the property in 1980. It is located one lot east of the twelve-story Augusta Landmark Hotel (1969), which provides a striking contrast between 19th and 20th century scale and design.

49

9. Old Medical College of Georgia, *598 Telfair Street*
(Charles B. Cluskey, 1835).

At the time of its design by Irish-born architect Charles B. Cluskey, the Medical College of Georgia building was one of the most complete expressions of the Greek Revival in Georgia. The brick walls, stuccoed and scored to imitate ashlar block, massive Doric columns, and crowning dome give the impression of permanence, undoubtedly a desirable effect for the fledgling institution in the 1830s.

The school moved to the former Augusta Orphan Asylum (1873, 1890) at Railroad and Harper Streets in 1913, and in 1928, the Sand Hills Garden Club began a campaign to refurbish this building as a community center. The brick wall surrounding the property replaces an original wooden fence.

Beginning in 1989, the building was renovated by the Medical College of Georgia Foundation, including new exterior stucco reproducing the original limestone color. Along with the Gertrude Herbert Institute of Art, the Augusta-Richmond County Museum, and the First Presbyterian Church, this building is part of the City of Augusta's first local historic preservation district (1974), which was established to preserve a three-block streetscape of Augusta's most prominent 19th century public buildings.

10. John Phinizy House, *519 Greene Street (about 1838).*

When the construction of the Greene Street median was nearly completed, merchant, banker, and Augusta Mayor (1837) John Phinizy built this townhouse nearly opposite the Augusta City Hall. Originally a two-story residence with unpainted brick, the building is raised over a high, finished basement. The entrance to the elevated main floor is through a Greek Revival portico flanked by a pair of elliptical stairways. The triple-ellipse window lintels were used in a number of other downtown buildings built in the 1830s and 1840s.

The Phinizy House is a conservative design resembling townhouses built in other East Coast port cities, including several in Savannah designed by Charles B. Cluskey.

53

11. Old Government House, *432 Telfair Street* *(1801, about 1848, 1989)*.

More than any other building, the Government House represents the history of the historic preservation movement in Augusta. About 1801, the original brick building was constructed as the home of local government. After city offices and the Richmond County Court were moved to Greene Street in 1820, the building became a private residence. The tall front facade windows flanking the central doorway are set in blind arches, the Federal detail used in three other prominent public buildings of the early 19th-century: St. Paul's Church, First Presbyterian Church and the Augusta City Courthouse.

The stuccoed facade, parapet, cast iron verandah, and matching wings were added about 1848. Despite an enclosed two-story rear porch and modern landscaping, the building still has the appearance of a fashionable suburban villa of the 1840s.

The building remained a private residence until 1954, when the Junior League of Augusta purchased the house for use as a reception center. The Government House became one of the most widely-used historic buildings of the 60s and early 70s. In 1972, Courthouse Lane, granite block-paved street immediately west of the building, was built under the auspices of Historic Augusta, Inc. The Street was part of an overall scheme to redevelop the block by renovating existing buildings and moving old buildings from other locations in the city.

12. Woodrow Wilson House, *419 Seventh (McIntosh) Street, (about 1859).*

Similar to the site of many Greene Street detached townhouses, this symmetrical, brick house sits on a small lot with a narrow front yard. The main open space is a backyard partially enclosed by the main house, a kitchen wing along Telfair Street and a carriage house. In 1901, a single-story porch was built across the front.

Owned by the nearby First Presbyterian Church from 1860-1930 and used as its parsonage, this house was a boyhood home of Woodrow Wilson, 28th President of the United States. The Reverend Joseph R. Wilson led the church and lived in its parsonage with his family from 1860 to 1870.

In 1991, Historic Augusta, Inc. purchased the property and began developing the building as a museum house.

57

13. Pullman Hall, *560 Walton Way (about 1856).*

The Central of Georgia, a line whose main branch began in Savannah and ran into Georgia's piedmont through Macon, was the Georgia railroad's main competition during the 1850s. After a 53-mile trunk line was established from Millen to Augusta about 1856 (originally the Augusta-Waynesboro Railroad), the company built this office building and adjoining freight shed. The straight-forward brick design with stone lintels and sills gives the office an aura of permanence and utility. Large wooden brackets help support the freight shed eaves and show the emerging taste for Italianate design.

After the mid 19th century, an industrial and warehouse district developed along the canal and railroads. This divided the main city north of Walker Street from less elaborate residential development south of present-day Walton Way (originally Calhoun Street).

The building was renovated in 1983 as Pullman Hall, a reception center. In 1989, the front facade was dramatically obscured by the construction of a railroad overpass along Walton Way.

14. Old Academy of Richmond County,
540 Telfair Street (1801, 1856).

At roughly the same time as the construction of the Government House, the Academy of Richmond County building was built on the undeveloped southern edge of the city.

The original building was remodeled with fortress-like battlements and a stucco facade about 1856 by builder William H. Goodrich. These Tudor Gothic details reflected the martial character of the male high school and were also used in the design of the munitions buildings built by the Confederate States of America government along the canal and at the United States Arsenal during the early 1860s.

The academy was moved to a new site at the intersection of Walton Way and Baker Avenue in 1929. Since then, the building has been used as a library and, (from 1960 until 1996) a local museum.

15. "P.G." Historic District,
(also referred to as Olde Towne since 1979).

Established on the eastern edge of the city early in the 19th century, this residential neighborhood is bounded by the river on the north, the Gordon Highway (1953-1957) on the west, East Boundary on the east, and Magnolia Cemetery, Cedar Grove Cemetery and May Park (once called the Parade Ground - a possible inspiration for the neighborhood's historic name) on the south.

Once the largest neighborhood of two-story, detached townhouses in Augusta, "P.G." has a variety of townhouse architecture built on narrow lots from the 1850s through the early-20th century. Although it is impossible to prove (since nearly half the area was burned in the large downtown fire of 1916), the mid-19th century houses of lower Broad and Greene were as elaborate as any in the city.

Clearly, the majority of the post-1916 replacements - including bungalows, foursquares, Mission, and other popular styles of the era - were more modest designs. On the southern and eastern fringe of the neighborhood along lower Telfair and Walker Street are the simplest

63

buildings, including shotgun houses and single-story cottages. Broad Street and Greene Street are distinguished by landscape medians, which were replanted after the 1916 fire.

Present-day landmarks include the Spanish Colonial revival Houghton School (1917), the Telfair Inn (a hotel complex located in a row of Victorian townhouses along the 300 block of Telfair Street and Greene Streets), and adjoining Cedar Grove Cemetery (public burial ground for blacks established about 1823).

In 1980, the area was listed on the National Register of Historic Places. This listing created the opportunity to use the federal tax incentives for renovation. Olde Towne has experienced a steady wave of renovation ever since.

16. The Augusta Canal *(1845-46, 1872-75).*

Following the early 19th century lead of other fall-line cities, local businessmen and the City of Augusta tried to revive a floundering local economy by constructing the seven-mile Augusta Canal from 1845 to 1846 as a source of power, a public water system, and a convenient route for shipping cargo from above the rocky shoals into the city.

In a later attempt to stimulate the local economy, mayor Charles Estes led the program to enlarge the canal from 1872 to 1875. This campaign occurred during one of the deepest national financial downturns of the 19th century.

The Augusta Canal led to the construction of housing for factory workers and commercial buildings for the cotton trade.

Today, a group of 19th century brick cotton mills and other smaller factories sit along the canal as far west as Harrisburg, where the King and Sibley mills create a dramatic architectural vista from upper Broad Street and the River Watch Parkway (1991). Beyond the Mill, the canal runs through undeveloped land until it meets the river between Interstate #20 and the Stevens Creek hydroelectric dam. The canal is still a source of hydroelectric power.

The industrial buildings lining the canal became part of a National Landmark historic district in 1971 (enlarged in 1976). In 1996, The Augusta Canal became a national heritage area, a new type of national park.

17. The Enterprise Mill, *1400 block Greene Street*
(1848 , 1877, Jones S. Davis, 1881).

The building on the south end of the Enterprise Mill (easily seen from the eastern end of the John C. Calhoun Expressway) is the 1848 Granite Mill, a flour mill built of locally-quarried granite. The main brick section of the Enterprise was built in 1877, then enlarged three years later to take advantage of the canal's enlarged power capacity.

The two prominent towers on the east facade are crowned with mansard roofs, the mark of the French Second Empire design universally popular for all types of building during the 1870s and 1880s.

The factory was built so the long range of windows facing east and west would maximize natural light and save on gas lighting. Once indispensable for ventilation, the arched window openings have been filled in, obscuring the dynamic rhythm of repetitive, multilight window sashes.

The mill complex was a textile operation until 1983, when the Graniteville Company ceased operation at this site.

1848, Granite Mill

69

18. The John P. King Manufacturing Co.,
1701 Goodrich Street, (John D. Hill, 1882).

This mill is another product of the industrial expansion following the 1875 enlargement of the canal. Although the original openings have been filled with brick, the central, Italianate brick tower displays its original design with white window sash, cast-iron cresting, and an interior stairway leading to a large bell.

The tower is regularly decorated for holidays: a large American flag flies for the 4th of July, and a lighted Christmas tree stands in December. Along with the Sibley Mill, the King Mill is a Harrisburg landmark, easily seen from the Calhoun Expressway, Broad Street, and the River Watch Parkway.

71

19. The Josiah Sibley Manufacturing Company,
1717 Goodrich Street (Jones S. Davis, 1880).

In terms of exterior decoration, the Sibley Mill is the most elaborate factory building in Augusta. In fact, when the construction of the Sibley Mill was completed, a group of company shareholders complained that the building design, its ornate brickwork and crenelations with Jacobean spires, was unnecessarily elaborate.

The Sibley Mill was built on the fomer site of the Confederate Powder Works (C. Shaler Smith, 1862, demolished, 1872). Commissioned by the young Confederate government, the Powder Works complex consisted of twenty buildings built along a two-mile section of the canal.

The sole surviving remnant of the Powder Works is a tapered chimney, which was originally built in front of a large refinery building. It was dedicated as a Confederate memorial in 1872.

20. Springfield Baptist Church, *114 Twelfth (Marbury) Street (about 1801 and 1897).*

This church complex is a landmark of upper Reynolds Street, the east-west avenue which divides the Riverfront development on the north and the Broad Street Historic Distric on the south.

The church complex is made up of two buildings: the late-nineteenth century brick sanctuary with twin towers facing Twelfth (Marbury) Street, and the early-nineteenth century frame parish hall, which was once an earlier sanctuary building. Built as a Methodist meeting house in 1801 for the St John's congregation on Greene Street, the parish hall was moved to this location in 1844, when St. John's built a new, brick church.

The Village of Springfield was located between Augusta and Harrisburg after the American Revolution, and was absorbed by the City of Augusta in 1798. This pioneering black Baptist Church is the proposed centerpiece of a new public park celebrating the church's rich history.

St. John Building, built as 1801 Methodist Meeting House.

21. Harrisburg Historic District

During the early-19th century, Harrisburg was a small rural village west of the city limits bounded by the river and vacant flatland which separated Augusta and Summerville.

The Ezekiel Harris House (see Site #67), the Mackay House, two ferry crossings to South Carolina, and two important rural roads were early landmarks in the area. The Harris plantation house was built near the intersection of the Washington Road- a western continuation of Broad Street - and the road to Summerville, known as the Sand Hills Road or Battle Row.

Buildings on village-size lots were generally clustered along the "Great Western Road", now Broad Street. By 1827, Harrisburg contained 40 houses, 6 stores, and a Presbyterian Church.

In 1873, a group of local businessmen led by J. J. Gregg and Mayor Charles Estes organized a real estate and building and loan association to develop 471 acres between Walton Way, Broad Street and the city limits. Organized along a grid street system and 40 to 60 foot wide lots, Harrisburg was transformed from a rural village into a mill-oriented suburb of single story frame cottages. The area was annexed to the city in 1882.

Although the Calhoun Expressway cut a swath through the area in 1973, Harrisburg retains most of its late-19th century ambiance.

The neighborhood was nominated to the National Register in 1990.

22. Shotgun House.

During the 1880s and 1890s, versions of this distinctly southern, urban design (single-story frame cottages with narrow front facades and rooms arrange in a single-row) were often built on narrow lots at the edge of the city in places like eastern "P.G.," Harrisburg, and Laney-Walker.

23. 1125-1135 Broad Street *(about 1915).*

This block of four three-story buildings symbolizes Augusta's burgeoning economy in the early 20th century. The first-floor commercial space and the two upper floors of residential flats are connected by an atrium for light and ventilation. Cast-iron columns along the first level facade were manufactured by the local Lombard Iron Works.

These buildings, with their continuous brick and sheet metal cornice and wrought iron balconies, are late examples of commercial town-houses in Augusta. When this block was built, the trend on the commercial blocks of Broad Street had shifted from mixed-use to single-use buildings. Examples of single-use buildings are furniture stores, department stores, banks, and office buildings.

24. Augusta Cotton Exchange, *801 Reynolds Street*
(E.W. Brown, 1886).

Built as the headquarters of The Exchange and Board of Trade, the official name of the group which represented Augusta's cotton factors, this building was conveniently located in the center of Augusta's cotton trading district. During the 19th and early 20th centuries, cotton factors and other merchants built offices and warehouses near the working waterfront. Buying cotton from piedmont planters for either shipment to the coast or use in the local textile mills was a major component of Augusta's 19th century commercial life.

The dynamic brick and stone design with a mansard roof (burned in the 1916 fire and replaced in 1989) was one of the most elaborate built in Augusta during the 1880s. Round and rectangular windows surrounded by stone lintels and sills, a Queen Anne corner turret with pseudo half-timbering supported by a cast-iron column (with its maker's mark "Geo. R. Lombard Iron Works. Augusta, GA 1886"), and incised Eastlake stone lintels made the building design very up-to-date in 1886.

After a 1989-1990 renovation, the Cotton Exchange has become the headquarters for the Augusta-Metropolitan Convention and Visitors Bureau. It marks the Eighth (Jackson) Street gateway to the Riverwalk, a pioneering cut in the levee, riverfront park, and esplanade.

25. Sacred Heart Cultural Center, *1301 Greene Street*
(Brother Cornelius Otten after Sacred Heart Church, Galveston, Texas,
Nicholas Clayton, 1898-1907).

With its soaring vertical architecture, Sacred Heart has been an
Augusta landmark since its turn-of-the-century construction as a
Roman Catholic Church. The church was closed in 1971.

The 1986 renovation earned developer Peter Knox the National Trust
for Historic Preservation's Outstanding Achievement Award. With its
cathedral-like design of twin turrets, Romanesque arches, decorative
brickwork, stained glass, and interior decorative painting, Sacred
Heart serves as a center for public receptions.

The prominent structure rises above the elevated eastern section of
the John C. Calhoun Expressway and acts as a monument to the
western edge of Augusta's 19th century development.

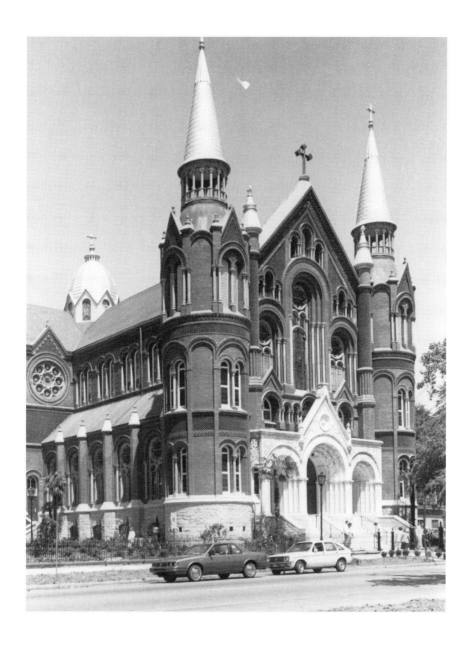

87

26. The Imperial Theatre *(G. Lloyd Preacher, 1918),*

The terra cotta facades of this early-20th century vaudeville and movie theatre is a vivid monument to downtown's traditional function as the city's entertainment center. Like permanent stage sets, the Imperial's facade designs was very up-to-date Commercial Gothic or represented an allusion to some far-off fantasy land.

The Imperial is currently in operation as a community theatre for the Augusta Ballet, Augusta Opera and other performance groups.

27. Laney-Walker Historic District.

As early as the mid-19th century, simple two-story frame buildings and cottages are scattered near Augusta's southern periphery along a street which has been called South Boundary, Gwinnett Street, and now Laney-Walker Boulevard. From 1850 through the 1880s, the area developed as the home of factory and railroad workers and, later, as the home of Augusta's black community.

From Walton Way south to the edge of the city, the Laney-Walker neighborhood developed along an extension of Augusta's street grid with closely spaced dwellings, factories along the canal, and early 20th century commercial buildings along Laney-Walker Boulevard.

The neighborhood bounded by Walton Way, Laney-Walker Boulevard, Twiggs Street, and Dent Boulevard was listed on the National Register of Historic Places in 1985.

28. Tabernacle Baptist Church, *1223 Laney-Walker Boulevard (1915).*

Founded by the Reverend Charles T. Walker, this church and its twin brick towers (capped with small neoclassical belfries similar to St. Paul's) are a landmark anchoring the western section of Laney-Walker Boulevard.

Located in a neighborhood of one- and two-story buildings, the large scale, detailing, and site directly on Laney-Walker Boulevard give this building a monumental presence.

This church, along with others in the neighborhood, have traditionally acted as multipurpose social and religious centers for the surrounding black community.

29. The Former University Hospital (*G. Lloyd Preacher and Meyer J. Sturn of Chicago, Consulting Architect, 1914, Demolished 1989-1991*)
The Medical College of Georgia Complex
(*between Walton Way, Thirteenth, and Fifteenth Street*).

When this city hospital was built in the relatively undeveloped southwest section of the city, the nearest landmarks were the Georgia railroad tracks and the Augusta Manufacturing Company, the city's first major cotton factory (1848, demolished early 1960s) which stood east of the intersection of the Augusta Canal and Thirteenth (McKinne) Street.

The design of the 325-bed hospital reflected the current taste for classically inspired public architecture and a system for separating patients into three building pavilions.

Today, a new University Hospital (Kulke, Wade, and Gauger, 1967), Veterans Administration Hospital (Abrew and Roberson, 1980), Talmadge Hospital (1950), and Medical College of Georgia campus create a distinct service district of mid-rise buildings located west of Laney-Walker, south of Walton Way and east of Fifteenth (Carnes) Street.

Former University Hospital

View From Summerville

30. Archibald Butt Memorial Bridge, *near the intersection of Greene and Fifteenth Streets at the Augusta Canal (W.H. Deacy, Architect; Nisbet Wingfield, Engineer; W.W. Leland Co., architectural decorations, 1914).*

Easily seen driving west on the John C. Calhoun Expressway, this small bridge is a picturesque example of early twentieth century public architecture. It was built as a memorial to Major Archibald W. Butt, an Augusta native and former aide to Presidents Teddy Roosevelt and William H. Taft. Major Butt died in the sinking of the luxury ocean liner Titanic on May 14, 1912.

Imitating the design of masonry bridges built from Roman times until the introduction of cast iron and steel, the bridge structure relies on three vaults supporting an arching roadway. It is decorated with concrete balustrades, decorative lions, and four Roman victory columns with eagles perched on globe lights. These neoclassical details seem well suited to the task of commemorating the life of a native hero.

A Georgia Department of Transportation plan to change the bridge led to the "Save Our Butt" movement in 1993.

31. U.S. Post Office and Courthouse, *100 E. Ford Street*
(Oscar Wenderoth, 1914, 1995-96)

Created as an early 20th century example of the city planning or City Beautiful movement, Barrett Plaza was the setting for Augusta's railroad station, Union Station (Francis Milburn, 1902), the ten-story Plaza Hotel (G. Lloyd Preacher, 1914), and this Italian Renaissance Revival federal building.

The U.S. Post Office and Courthouse building was designed by Oscar Wenderoth, an architect who had trained with Carrerre and Hastings, the New York firm nationally known for their Beaux-Arts commissions. In 1912, President Taft appointed Wenderoth head of the U.S. Supervising Architect's Office, where his main responsibility was to design federal post office buildings.

Typical of the Renaissance Revival, each floor has a different window design. The multicolored terra cotta cornice brackets, cast iron fan-light grills, and red barrel-tile roof give texture to an otherwise low-relief exterior design. The building stands out as one of the most sophisticated examples of public architecture in the city.

When Union Station was demolished in the 1960s (and likewise The Plaza (James) Hotel in 1991), this public square lost its focal point, and in many ways, its public purpose.

32. The Lamar Building, *753 Broad Street*
(1916, WL Stoddard of NY and G. Lloyd Preacher).

The Lamar Building's sixteen-story, steel-frame, brick and structural terra cotta construction, which was begun in 1913, was an optimistic project for the building's developer, the Empire Life Insurance Company of Atlanta. At the time, Augusta had only four miles of paved streets and most residents travelled by streetcar. The insurance company was bankrupt before construction was complete.

The Lamar Building's facade is a theatrical collection of historical references. A recessed Doric Portico anchors a two story base. The building's main shaft is a combination of Commercial Gothic and Italianate details cast in terra cotta. Above the major building setback at floor 13, the tower rises the final 4 floors to an exuberant, multi-colored, palazzo-style cornice. High-relief, terra cotta crestings are also found on the Chronicle (Herald) Building (1920, G. Lloyd Preacher), the Richmond Summit Apartments 1924 (originally the Richmond Hotel), and the Marion Building (Chronicle Building, 1914).

In 1973, State Senator Eugene Holley commissioned the nationally-recognized IM Pei and Partners firm to replace the original red tile pyramid-shaped roof with a two-story penthouse. The abstract design of smooth, geometric shapes is a stark contrast to the original building's high-relief detailing.

In 1978, the building was listed on the National Register of Historic Places. A renovation begun in 1986 has made the Lamar Building's interior, above the historic lobby, one of the newest in downtown Augusta.

100

33. Y.M.C.A. Building, *945 Broad Street*
(Scroggs and Ewing, 1926).

The present building was built on the site of the Planter's Hotel, the early 19th century landmark of Broad Street's western commercial development and one of the city's largest antebellum buildings. Originally home to the Y.M.C.A., this building was renovated as offices and a health club in 1985 as part of a $9 million adaptive-use project by Bankers First. The row of 19th century buildings in the center of the block is bounded on the west by the marble bank building built for First Federal Savings and Loan (Kuhlke and Wade, 1959).

The neo-Georgian facade of the Y.M.C.A. building has red brick upper floors built above a cut stone base. The design takes advantage of its corner site on Macartan Street with a second-story terrace connecting two wings of the building. During the renovation, landscape architect Robert Marvin designed Lafayette Plaza, a large, naturalistic courtyard in the rear of the adjacent 19th century buildings. Before the 1986 renovation, the Jones Street entrance to 949 Broad Street (about 1830) was through an arched passageway running through a two-story carriage house mews.

34. Augusta-Richmond County Municipal Building,
530 Greene Street (Scroggs and Ewing, Kuhlke and Wade, 1957).

Serious and straightforward, the fortresslike design of this government office building is a nine-story central block recessed behind a pair of three-story wings. The decoration is confined to the regular repetition of windows separated by granite panels and vertical marble strips. Sheets of marble surrounding each window give the facade the look of strength.

This monumental quality of the front facade along Greene Street is reinforced by Monument Street. This two-block street was created in the 1850s to provide a vista of the seat of local government from Broad Street and the newly erected Signer Monument.

This austerc building replaced the 1820 brick Richmond County Courthouse, which was demolished. "Blind Justice," the allegorical statue which crowned the neo-classical cupola of the earlier building, now sits at the south entrance to the building.

35. First Union (Georgia Railroad Bank) Building,

796 Broad Street (Robert McCreary, Architect; Patchen and Mingledorf, Engineers, 1968).

Rising seventeen stories in the center of the Broad Street commercial district, the building helps define the local skyline and, with its corporate logo, is one of Augusta's most easily recognized commercial landmarks. A smooth glass and dark metal curtain-wall was the stylish design for professional office tower after Ludwig Mies van der Rohe's created his trend-setting design for the Seagrams Building (1958) in New York City.

A year after the construction of the First Union Building, another bank and office tower, the fourteen-story Trust Company Building (now SunTrust Building) was built one corner west. Built with a larger palette of materials, glass, concrete, stone aggregate, and marble, the facade of the Trust Company Building is unrestrained compared to the glass and metal curtain-walls typical of corporate design in the 1960s.

36. Augusta-Richmond County Civic Center,
601 Seventh Street, (I.M. Pei and Associates, 1979).

During the 1960s and 1970s, large civic centers for all types of entertainment were typical construction projects aimed at revitalizing cities across the country.

Augusta's version was built on a former industrial site, the Georgia Railroad's roundhouse, foundry and repair yard south of Barrett Plaza (1911) and the Bell Auditorium (1937, Scroggs and Ewing).

The design relies mainly on the building shape: a large horizontal block elevated over a smaller base. Its gray, nearly sheer, metal panels are uninterrupted by windows and are decorated only by a repeating pattern of squares and triangles. The elevated main entrance facade along Eighth Street is located diagonally to the street and is high-lighted by three red awnings.

The Suburbs

II. The Suburbs

37. Summerville Historic District.

About 1800, John Milledge, Thomas Cumming, and George Walton all owned tracts of pine land on the 300-foot-high ridge west of Augusta. Each subdivided and sold parcels for the construction of summer houses. Walton's 250 acres, however, ultimately developed as the heart of antebellum Summerville.

The center of the grid street plan was the intersection of Milledge Road and Walton Way, (in the 18th century, a "way" was a thorough-fare running through private land), and Walton's lots extended from Hickman Road on the east to Johns Road on the west. During the warm months from March to October, town-dwellers migrated to the nearby ridge to avoid the threat of warm weather fevers. Battle Row was the only road to Summerville until 1850, when Walton Way was extended from the present-day curve at the intersection of Hickman Road west to the city's western boundary at Fifteenth Street (Carnes Road).

The neighborhood's earliest houses were wooden and, in most respects, resembled farmhouses. Raised cottages and simple two story buildings had full-width porches, often with views of the city three miles east. While unpaved, the streets of Summerville were often given a linear precision through the construction of wooden fences along front property lines.

Before the mid 19th century, the only brick buildings in Summerville

were built at the United States Arsenal. Situated on the former site of a small plantation west of the village center, the quadrangle of military buildings was initially the object of protest by residents, but eventually its well-planned, low-density ground blended with the village's suburban character.

Beginning in the late 1840s, suburban villas reflecting the national taste for Greek Revival and Italianate designs were built. In 1850, the connection of Walton Way to the city along a plank road made daily commuting possible. In 1866, a mule-drawn trolley was established along this route. By the time the Georgia Legislature established the Village of Summerville in 1861, many seasonal residents were used year-round.

In 1890, two events heralded a period of expanded suburban growth in Summerville. Electric streetcar service replaced the mule-powered trolleys and the Bon Air, the first and most prominent of a group of local winter resort hotels, completed its first winter season. The convenience and speed of the streetcar system, and then the automobile, created new demand for suburban residences on "the Hill." Private land was constantly subdivided, especially on the southern and western edges of the antebellum village.

Summerville expanded with the creation of new subdivisions like Monte Sano (1890, 1900 along with Monte Sano and both sides of Central Avenue) and Harison Heights (1895, along McDowell and Kings Way west of Johns Road). Boulevards with landscaped medians, like Henry Street and Central Avenue, created a visible focus for new residential construction.

Repeated flooding downtown and the great fire of 1916 accelerated the residential trend from the city and to the suburbs. Insurance claims from lost property downtown often were reinvested in new Summerville homes.

During the 1920s and 1930s local architects such as Harry Wendell, G. Lloyd Preacher, Lynn Drummond, Willis Irvin, Philetus Scroggs and Whitney Ewing designed "period houses", interpretations of historical American and European houses, for construction on new residential lots.

This amalgamation of post-1890 suburban architecture built around a small antebellum summer colony was designated the Summerville National Register Historic District in 1980.

38. 914 Milledge Road *(about 1800).*

Built close to Milledge Road and standing behind a hedge of yaupon holly, this is one of Summerville's earliest and best known examples of a Sand Hills cottage. Built as a summer retreat, this house represents the traditional, often rural character of many antebellum Summerville houses.

Although hardly uniform, a Sand Hills cottage usually featured a high brick basement, a story-and-a-half frame section, dormer windows, and simple front and rear porches. The origin of the raised cottage has never been fully documented, but the West Indies and its lucrative late-18th century sugar maritime trade is the likely inspiration for this building type.

In Summerville, early 19th century cottages had simple interior detailing and furnishings. The modest summer house designs were replaced by larger and more elaborate dwellings throughout the antebellum period. From 1850 to 1870, for instance, Greek Revival and Italianate designs, the first national styles for house-building, began to outnumber these vernacular cottages.

During the peak of the winter tourist era, 1890 to 1930, several Sand Hills cottages were renovated as part of the national interest in "colonial" architecture.

39. Barna McKinne House, *2229 Pickens Road (about 1810).*

This early summer house faced Milledge Road on a three-acre site (lot #25 in George Walton's subdivision plan) from the time of its construction for merchant Barna McKinne around 1810 until it was rolled on logs to its Pickens Road about 1890.

The trellise-porch decoration was made by a stream-powered jigsaw and was the wooden counterpart of contemporary cast iron porches. This design was a popular feature used by local builder William H. Goodrich, who probably added the porch and wings in the mid 19th century.

40. Augusta State University (U.S. Arsenal), *2500 Walton Way (about 1828).*

Built in Summerville to avoid its previous, unhealthy site near the river, the United States Arsenal was established during the late 1820s on a seventy-two-acre section of the Bellvue plantation.

East of the quadrangle is the original Bellvue plantation house, an early 19th century raised cottage with Victorian-era exterior shingling, brick chimneys, and millwork. In 1957, the Arsenal became the campus of Augusta College. Sixteen single-story barracks were joined and faced with brick to create eight new classroom buildings. Extensive parking lots and two institutional buildings of the 1970s, the Reese Library and the Maxwell Performing Arts Center, now compete with the antebellum quadrangle buildings as the dominant architecture of the suburban campus. The name of the institution was changed to Augusta State University in 1996.

41. 708 Milledge Road *(about 1830 with mid l9th century additions).*

This early, two-story summer house stands at the intersection of Milledge and Battle Row (sometimes called simply the Sand Hills Road), the rural road which alone connected Summerville with Harrisburg and Augusta before 1850. The paired columns, jigsawed arches, and crowning balustrade of the wraparound veranda are an interpretation of an Italian loggia executed in wood.

The simple, horizontal board fence was a common Summerville feature during the 19th century.

42. Appleby Library, 2260 Walton Way *(about 1838, Henry Wendell, 1910).*

This branch of the Augusta-Richmond County Library system sits at the corner of Walton Way and Johns Road, at the western edge of the 250 acres which George Walton subdivided to create Summerville. The crook in the road is the result of the 18th century boundary between Walton's land and a large tract owned by Frances Willis.

Built for Judge Benjamin Warren, the front and side facades are typical solutions to fusing the design of an unpretentious two-story farm house-type building with the spirit of the Greek revival. The front, two-story Doric columns support an architrave, but no pediment. Instead, the roof gables on the east and west side of the house have been transformed into pediments. The rear facade is part of an early 20th century renovation attributed to local architect, Henry T.E. Wendell.

In 1954, the Appleby family donated the property for use as a public library. Despite its public use, the property has retained its original residential character and is the site for a summer series of outdoor concerts.

Kitchen Outbuilding

124

43. The Alan Fuqua Center ("Montrose"), *2249 Walton Way (1848).*

Although this former residence is a story-and a half building raised over a finished brick basement, its scale and degree of detail far exceeds most Sand Hills cottages built in antebellum Summerville. The temple portico, for example, is a full-blown expression of the Greek Revival. And its cast iron balconies and column capitals represent the appearance of pioneering iron foundries in the 1840s.

The suburban villa was built for lawyer Robert A. Reid, whose 1876 bequest helped establish the Reid Memorial Presbyterian Church. The church complex is located on the western edge of the original property.

In 1974, the house was named the Alan Fuqua center and is used as a reception and meeting center for the adjacent church.

Northwest of the house is a one-story, brick, octagonal kitchen building. Like another example at 812 Milledge Road, the building represents the short-lived national fad for octagonal building design in the late 1840s and 1850s.

Octagonal Kitchen Outbuilding

44. Charles J. Jenkins House ("Green Court"), *2248 Cumming Road (about 1830 and 1859).*

In the mid 1850s, lawyer Charles J. Jenkins, State Supreme Court Justice and later Georgia's first postbellum Governor, bought this house, which was advertised for sale in the June 8, 1854 Augusta Citizen and Sentinel as "the Sand Hills Residence of Mrs. Eliz. Reid, usual outbuildings, stables, 4 & 1/2 acres, improved Gardens and Fruit Trees."

Jenkins commissioned builder William H. Goodrich to convert the exterior into an up-to-date Italianate villa, with wide, bracketed eaves and a trellise-design veranda which nearly surrounded the house. The porch is one of the largest in Georgia and is decorated with both wooden and cast iron details. The wooden details were undoubtedly manufactured by steam-powered jigsaw located at Goodrich's mill on Reynolds Street.

On 1910, Henry P. Crowell of Chicago, President of the Quaker Oats company, purchased the house as his winter residence, named it "Green Court," and established one of Summerville's most elaborate formal gardens. The house immediately east was built as the residence of Mr. Crowell's gardener and designed by Henry T.E. Wendell. The western section of the garden along Johns Road was subdivided into four house lots in the 1960s.

45. "Gould's Corner." 828 Milledge Road *(about 1859)*.

This Italianate villa was built for merchant Artemas Gould, a native of Massachusetts, by professional builder William H. Goodrich. The cube-shaped house, crowned with an octagonal cupola, is an example of the national building style which gradually surpasses the popularity of the Greek Revival during the 1850s.

The villa style entry portico with its paired columns, cast iron Corinthian capitals, and a crowning balustrade contrasts with the full width, two-story, rear veranda.

In the early 1970's, a group of neighbors purchased the house to prevent its demolition. The renovation meant dividing the house into three, full-floor condominiums and constructing eight attached townhouses in the rear.

Condominiums at rear of property

46. Redmond-Hickman House, *956 Hickman Road (1861).*

The design for this summer house lies somewhere between pattern book recommendations for an ornamental farmhouse and a suburban villa. The steep roof, central gable, and board and batten siding emphasize Gothic verticality, while the crowning cupola is a standard feature of Italianate villas.

The house was built for Dennis Redmond, the editor of the local agricultural newspaper *The Southern Cultivator* and founder of "Fruitland" (see Site #74) on the eve of the Civil War. Redmond terraced the sloping site on the brow of the Summerville ridge for a vineyard.

During the ownership of Graniteville Mill President Hamilton H. Hickman, from 1872 to 1904, the property was expanded to forty eight acres, most of which were later subdivided into new suburban lots along Heard Avenue and Russell Street after Hickman's death in 1904.

Pendant roof detail

The two-story rear porch commands a view of the city and, during the 19th century, was a landmark for travelers ascending the Walton Way hill from Augusta to Summerville.

47. The Church of the Good Shepherd, *2230 Walton Way (John J. Nevitt of Philadelphia, 1880; MacMurphy and Story, 1898).*

Like an English parish church, this small-scale, High Victorian Gothic church helped mark the center of late 19th century Summerville.

The Good Shepherd's dynamic polychrome facade, created by the use of a multicolored roof slate and brick, was built before the return of classicism at the turn of the century. The location of the bell tower near the transept, rather than above the main entrance, gives the design its asymmetrical roofline and picturesque character. The steep pitch of the main roof, the vestibule roofs at each entrance, and the belfry roof give the design a Gothic verticality.

In typical 19th century taste, a cast-iron fence marked the front line until the last two decades. Near its western boundary, a Sand Hills cottage, called "Azalea Cottage", stood until 1969, when it was moved to the entrance of Rockbrook, a Berckmans Road subdivision just beyond the city limits. An "Azalea Cottage" outbuilding, with board and batten siding and a jigsawed vergeboard typical of Carpenter Gothic design, stands west of the church. The mid 19th century Langdon House stood on the east at the corner of Walton Way and Milledge Road until 1969 when it was also moved to Berckmans Road, near Rae's Creek.

Instead of 19th century residences, the church is now flanked by two institutional buildings of the late 1960s: the round sanctuary of the Woodlawn Methodist Church (E.L. Perry, 1968) and the Episcopal Day School (Dort Payne, 1969, Gothic Revival renovations, Cheatham, Fletcher, Scott and Sears 1993).

Episcopal Day School

48. Central Avenue/Monte Sano Avenue *(about 1890).*

These two streets were created to accommodate the new electric streetcar line which began operation on Walton Way after 1890. The line brought passengers to the new layer of Summerville development, named Monte Sano, where a wide variety of bungalows, "four squares," and other early 20th century residential styles were built. For five cents, a passenger could ride from downtown to Summerville in fifteen minutes. Colonel Daniel B. Dyer, representing the Jarvis Conklin investment company of Kansas City, owned the network of streetcar lines in Augusta and was half-owner of the Monte Sano subdivision. About 1900, Colonel Dyer built an amusement park at the southwest corner of Central and Monte Sano Avenues with the dual purpose of attracting more people to ride the streetcar line and view new suburban lots.

The designs used in Monte Sano are similar to those built in "P.G." now called Olde Towne, after the 1916 fire.

In 1920, the City of Augusta planted the area along the streetcar tracks on Central Avenue from Monte Sano Avenue to Troup Street with oak trees as a memorial to World War I soldiers. The landscaped median is called Heroes Grove.

49. The Bon Air, 2101 Walton Way *(Willis Irvin and McKim, Meade and White of New York, 1923).*

The Bon Air sits in a landscaped park at the crest of the Summerville ridge. The original, frame Bon Air opened as a winter tourist hotel in 1889 (MacMurphy and Story, Architects). The six-story frame building featured Queen Ann turrets, a hydraulic elevator which ran from the ground floor to a third-floor solarium, and full-width front porches with panoramic views of the city and the South Carolina ridge north of the river.

The hotel was an instant success and became the center of Augusta's winter resort-business for fifty years. After a fire destroyed an enlarged version of the frame building in 1921, one of the nation's most prominent architectural firms designed the present Bon Air building as a palatial Mediterranean villa with stucco walls and a red Spanish tile roof. The resort business, however, didn't survive World War II.

The Bon Air is now apartments for the elderly, and together with the Partridge Inn and the George Walton condominiums, acts as the architectural gateway to Summerville.

50. North Augusta, South Carolina, *(1890, incorporated 1906).*

In 1890, a group of New York and Atlanta investors, organized as the North Augusta Land Company, bought 5000 acres across the river from Augusta and began developing North Augusta.

The developers built a steel bridge from Thirteenth (McKinne) Street across the Savannah in 1891, built a railroad spur from Hamburg (which had declined to the point of near-extinction by this time), and extended the street car line up the hill. The North Augusta Land Company laid out a complete town: industrial sites were located for a mile along the river, a commercial center between two public squares was located at the plateau of the first hill, residential lots were established on three sides of the commercial center, and a system of parks were planned on low-lying land throughout the town.

In 1895, Walter M. Jackson, built a monumental new-classical house, "Look-Away Hall", on the lot where two major street, Georgia Avenue and Carolina Avenue, merge. The town's larger houses, like James U. Jackson's "Rosemary Hall" on Carolina Avenue, were built on the hill rising above Calhoun Park, the triangular park with its Confederate monument sitting in front of "Look-Away Hall".

By 1901, 150 houses had been built in North Augusta, and in 1906 the town was incorporated.

In 1903, the Hampton Terrace, a 300-room winter resort hotel, was established near the top of the ridge, a location similar to that of the Bon Air in Summerville. After the frame hotel burned without insurance in 1910, however, the North Augusta development lost its momentum and regained it only as a 1950's automobile suburb during the construction of the Savannah River Plant.

51. The Partridge Inn, *2110 Walton Way (1899: G. Lloyd Preacher, 1907; Willis Irvin, 1929).*

The success of the nearby Bon Air caused Innkeeper Morris Partridge repeatedly to enlarge an early 19th century, frame Summerville residence from 1899 to 1929 as a tourist hotel. The twin Italianate towers and multi-storied front porch give the front facade a casual, picturesque character.

The Partridge Inn was renovated from 1983 to 1986, and serves the same two uses for which it was built: a main floor restaurant and upper-floor hotel rooms.

52. "Morningside," *606 Milledge Road (Kemp and Wedell, 1909).*

One of Summerville's largest winter resort homes, "Morningside" was built for Frank H. Denny of Pittsburgh about 1909, but soon became the home of Alfred S. Bourne, a New York attorney and charter member of the Augusta National Golf Club.

The gambrel roof, second floor shingles, and shed dormers were popular during the early-twentieth-century Dutch Colonial Revival, but the entire design hardly fits into any neat category. The house's asymmetry is created by a pair of stucco, two-story gables with battered walls, and a two-story entrance bay with a Palladian window providing natural light to the main staircase. The house resembles a seaside resort cottage as much as an affluent suburban villa.

Bourne Place now separates the main house from an elaborate garage and leads to a modern cul-de-sac of ranch houses which replaced a large section of "Morningside's" extensive gardens. Although the grounds have been drastically reduced in size, the house still sits in a private setting screened from Milledge Road.

53. Bungalow, *2623 Raymond Avenue (about 1920).*

Bungalows, probably the largest category of historic buildings in Georgia, are found in nearly every early-20th century suburb in the city. Usually single story, the design of these dwellings rely on the motifs and materials associated with the Arts and Crafts movement, rather than on a re-interpretation of an established historical style.

54. Augusta Fire Department Engine Company #7, *2163 Central Avenue (Thomas H. Campbell, 1914).*

In this building, the requirements of a neighborhood fire station are effectively blended with a popular building style of the 1910s, Mission Revival. The pair of scalloped parapets, each with a roof-covered balcony and terra cotta cartouches, identify the firemen's second-story dormitory and the two first-floor engine bays. The red tile roof and simple, central arcade complete the design.

Located prominently on a pie-slice shaped lot at the intersection of Central Avenue, Kings Way, and Troupe Street (whose extension, Kissingbower Road, connects South Augusta with Summerville, the building is a well-maintained example of distinctive public architecture.

55. George R. Stearns House, *704 Milledge Road, (Kemp and Wendell, 1909).*

Commissioned by Riverside Mill President George R. Stearns, This house design features a red tile roof, balconies, and scalloped end parapets, all elements of the Spanish Colonial Revival which swept the southern United States from Florida to California during the early 20th Century. The prominent parapet end walls are balanced by the central three-story tower incorporating the front door, a second floor balcony, and a third-floor Moorish window.

The house was built on a full-block site bounded by Milledge Road, Gardner Street, Gary Street, and Battle Row. The carriage house located near the rear of the original property has been cleverly converted into a modern residence and is surrounded by a good example of contemporary suburban landscaping. This picturesque Milledge Road site is surrounded by 19th and early 20th century suburban houses, cottages, and resort homes.

56. "Twin Gables," *920 Milledge Road (Wendell and Kemp, 1911).*

In the reigning fashion for country-house trappings, the elaborate winter houses built in Summerville from 1900 to 1930 often were christened with picturesque names. "Twin Gables" was built for Frances Hardy, a winter tourist from Chicago, and named for its symmetrical pair of shingled, gambrel-roof gables. The central section of the house is anchored by an Italian Renaissance-style entrance terrace. The house sits on a large lot created by merging two smaller lots initially developed in the 1880's. Surrounded by a brick wall (laid in Flemish bond with dark headers matching the house and St. Paul's Church), the grounds have ornamental terraces on the east and a pair of matching garden houses in the rear.

Since 1985, this house has been the official residence of the Medical College of Georgia president. The college has conducted an extensive program aimed at refurbishing the house and grounds. The front brick wall, adjoining sidewalk, and aggregate stone driveway are products of this recent project.

57. "Salubrity Hall," *2259 Cumming Road (Scroggs and Ewing, 1929).*

In 1929, winter resident Mrs. John W. Herbert commissioned this interpretation of an English Tudor-era house and its extensive formal gardens, tea house, and matching garage. The front facade design is based on a variety of gables creating an asymmetrical roofline. Covered with both brick and half-timbering, the exterior creates the picturesque effect of a 16th century English country house built and enlarged over a period of time.

This house is an important part of the resort-era winter residences which are concentrated along Milledge Road. While a large portion of the original gardens have been replaced by modern suburban lots on Montrose Court, the house design and large-scale grounds is similar to 1920s country-house building located in the affluent suburbs of nearly all large American cities.

Former Tea cottage on Montrose Court

58. Forrest Hills *(Hare and Hare, Landscape Architects, 1926; Blanchard and Calhoun, Developers)*

The Forrest Hills neighborhood was designed by Kansas City land planner S. Herbert Hare as a naturalistic automobile suburb.

The Darlington oaks lining the curving brick-paved streets and utility lines built along rear property lines define the carefully-planned character of the neighborhood. Park Avenue, a short straight street with a wide, landscaped median, was planned as a vista street leading to the park-like setting of the six-story Forrest Hills-Ricker Hotel (Demolished 1988, see site #59).

At the start of the 1929 depression, construction of new houses stalled and the resort hotel struggled for success. Still, throughout the 1930s, many of Augusta's finest examples of "period houses" - interpretations of historical precedent from both the United States and Europe - were designed by local architects like Lynn Drummond, Philetus Scroggs, and Willis Irvin in Forrest Hills.

In the early 1950s, the design of new subdivisions located beyond the western edge of the city, especially along Walton Way Extension, followed the lead of Forrest Hills' naturalistic street plan.

Today, the canopy of mature street trees casting shadows on the brick-paved streets is a dramatic example of public landscaping setting the tone for a residential neighborhood.

59. Forrest Hills-Ricker Hotel, *(Willis Irvin, Pringle and Smith of Atlanta, 1927; demolished 1988).*

This winter resort hotel was built on one of the city's highest elevations in a wooded area west of Summerville. The austere, low relief classical facade was built on axis with Park Avenue and was an integral part of the Forrest Hills development. Like the Bon Air, which Willis Irvin also helped design, the front facade was anchored by an elevated, balustrade enclosed terrace set behind a central port-cochere.

The hotel had 280 guest rooms and was surrounded by a 600 acre park including an 18 hole golf course (Donald Ross, Architect) in the rear and, at one time, tennis courts on its front lawn.

The resort business declined in the 1930s and, in 1942, the United States Army requisitioned the building as an army hospital. In 1950, the Veterans Administration re-named it Oliver General Hospital, a name it held until its abandonment in 1986.

159

60. Kilpatrick House, *1314 Comfort Road (late 18th century and early 19th century, renovation architect, Lynn Drummond, 1928).*

Once known as the Mansion House hotel, this house was moved from its original downtown site. A sign of the residential decline of downtown was the disassembly and relocation of this building from the southwest corner of Greene and Seventh Streets to this lot in suburban Forest Hills in 1928.

Raised on a finished brick basement with an elevated portico entrance similar to the Phinizy House (Site #10), the townhouse transplanted-to-the-suburbs has a transitional architectural personality. The entrance fanlight, delicate portico columns and double horse shoe are typical late Federal-era features, while the flat, two story pilasters and frieze with attic vents are expressions of the Greek Revival. This combination suggest that the final design was achieved in at least two distinct stages.

61. John Walton House, *3106 Walton Way Extension (about 1935).*

Set on a rolling, park-like lot, this temple-front house is a paragon of traditional suburban taste: neoclassical architecture incorporated into a bucholoc, naturalistic setting. The fluted Doric columns were salvaged from a burnt house on the southwest corner of Milledge and Cumming Road (Henry Cumming House, 1828).

When this house was built, there were only a few houses standing beyond the city limits on Walton Way Extension.

62. Julian Smith Casino, *Broad Street at Lake Olmstead (Lynn Drummond, 1937)*

Lake Olmstead, originally name Lake Rae, was created in 1873 during the enlargement of the Augusta Canal and the damming of Rae's Creek. By the beginning of the 20th century, the local electric street car system had a spur to Lakeview, a park with on the banks of the lake.

Commissioned by the City of Augusta, this rubble stone and log building is the headquarters of Julian Smith Park. Known for his suburban design, Lynn Drummond designed this enclosed pavilion to symbolize a naturalistic park created as an escape for downtown and suburban dwellers.

165

63. Murray Hill, *Walton Way Extension,*
(Sherman and Hemstreet realtors, 1952).

This charactcristic subdivision of the 1950s is built around a series of winding roads which reflect the rolling topography of the site. The naturalistic design is generally continued in the fence-less yards filled with tall pine trees, dogwoods, and azaleas.

Generally, single story ranch houses popular during the 1950s and 60s were built on quarter-acre lots. The entire formula was repeated several times in a series of subdivisions established along Walton Way Extension, and new suburban areas along major roads in metropolitan Augusta.

64a. Augusta Mall, *3450 Wrightsboro Road, (The Rouse Company 1978, expanded 1990);*
64b. The Regency Mall *(Edward J. DeBartolo Company, 1978)*

On July 27, 1978, The Regency Mall - at the time, Georgia's largest enclosed mall with over a million square feet - opened on a 75 acre site at the intersection of the Gordon Highway and Highway 1. The mall was designed to accommodate three anchor department stores and 139 other stores.

A week later another regional mall, the Augusta Mall, opened at the intersection of the Wrightsboro Road and Bobby Jones Expressway (Augusta's beltway which currently runs from Washington Road in Martinez to the New Savannah Road in South Augusta) with two anchor department stores and 109 smaller stores. Approximately half the size of the Regency Mall, the original Augusta Mall featured a central, two-story glass-covered arcade connecting the anchor stores. A "food court" doubles as the main entrance, and a glass elevator, fountain and an early 20th century street clock relocated from Broad Street, are highlights of the public space. Later expansions finished in 1990 meant the construction of two additional department stores.

Both malls are new centers of area shopping whose creation changed the character of the traditional downtown and prompted efforts to revitalize Broad Street and the riverfront.

Augusta Mall

Regency Mall

The Countryside

III. The Countryside

65. Stallings Island, *in the Savannah River 8 miles upstream from Augusta between the hydroelectric dam at Big Stevens Creek and the Augusta Canal lock and dam.*

This small, wooded island is known for its large Indian Mound (approximately 500 feet by 300 feet by 22 feet high) containing the artifacts of Indian culture beginning about 2700 B.C. These include pottery shards, game and fish bones, shells, arrow and knife heads, and clay pits associated with crude dwellings. The island has been excavated by amateurs and professional since the late 19th century. Excavations were conducted by William H. Claflin, Jr. of Bellmont, Massachusetts and Mr. and Mrs. C.B. Cosgrove of Harvard's Peabody Museum from 1908 to 1929.

A rare local landmark of pre-European culture, the site became a National Historic Landmark in 1966.

66. "Meadow Garden," *1320 Independence Drive*
(formerly Nelson Street, about 1792).

Built in the early 1790s for Virginia-born George Walton (formerly a Georgia Governor and signer of the Declaration of Independence), this raised cottage is one of the best local examples of late 18th century rural building. "Meadow Garden" was built on a rural site nearly a mile west of 18th century Augusta development. By giving his home a name, Walton followed the practice of 18th century Virginians.

The original house, currently the southern part of the structure, had two, main floor rooms called the hall and parlor. The building was enlarged to its present size about 1810. Contrasting with the simple exterior details, the original interior rooms have high-style Georgian overmantel paneling and wainscoting.

In 1990, the Georgia Chapter of the Daughters of the American Revolution bought the house and made it Georgia's first house museum. A renovation about 1900 incorporated two contrasting rooflines, representing the two stages of construction, into a unified design.

"Meadow Garden" now sits almost hidden off Thirteenth Street in a district dominated by the Augusta canal, industry, and the Medical College complex.

67. Ezekiel Harris Plantation, *1822 Broad Street (about 1797).*

At the end of the 18th century, this plantation house, with hints of both high style and frontier vernacular design, was built for tobacco planter and trader Ezekiel Harris.

The house was built facing the river near the intersection of two important early roads: the road leading west from Broad Street to Washington, Wilkes County (Washington road) and the road to Summerville (Battle Row). Closer to the river, Harris had a brick tobacco warehouse near a ferry crossing to Campbellton, S.C.

The area became an early 19th century rural village and, after 1873, a mill-oriented suburb. The Ezekiel Harris House now faces the canal and cotton mills, the centers of the industrial economy which replaced the rural one for which this house was built.

The defining feature of this house is the gambrel roof which covers front and rear two-story porches. The roofline, as well as some high style interior paneling, transforms the house from a standard, frontier farmhouse into a building with high style pretensions.

In 1948, the Richmond County Historical Society purchased the White House, as it was called, and in 1956 transferred the property to the State of Georgia. In 1964, the house was called the Mackey House when the Georgia Historical Commission completed a full-scale restoration program. The Ezekiel Harris House is now a house museum owned by the City of Augusta and operated by Historic Augusta, Inc.

68. Turknett Springs House, "Fairveiw" *2116 Wrightsboro Road (about 1797).*

Built on a 100-acre rural tract south of Summerville alongside the Wrightsboro Road, the house is a member of the small group of late 18th century buildings still standing in Augusta.

Like the Ezekiel Harris House, the two-story porch is an integral part of the building design. Simple, round columns resting in balustrade-high bases support seven elliptical arches. This design is further decorated by a delicate sheaf-of-wheat balustrade, a striking rural interpretation of Federal era neoclassical design.

The Turknett Springs House faces southeast toward the city and, like many early Summerville houses, was built with a view of the city.

179

69. Goodale Plantation, *Sand bar Ferry Road*
(Late 18th century and mid 19th century).

Located near the river facing the Sand Bar Ferry road to Beech Island, South Carolina, this plantation house shares the fate of other early houses built near the city on rural sites. The use of the surrounding land has changed, contrasting the house with its current environment. Since the 1960s, nearby rural land has been converted into an industrial, commercial, and residential district.

The house design is a blend of town and country features. Its off-center front door representing an interior side hall plan, for instance, is typical of townhouses built on narrow town lots. Furthermore, its overall brick construction, the parapet connecting the chimneys on the west hall, and the narrow front wall resemble many mid-19th-century commercial townhouses on Broad Street.

70. Hammond Plantation, *908 W. Martintown Road,*
North Augusta, South Carolina (early and mid 19th century).

Built on a hill facing Martintown Road, the late 18th century road from Augusta into the Edgefield District and piedmont South Carolina, the Hammond Plantation is a good example of early 19th century plantation construction. The original two-story, one-room-deep structure was built throughout the rural South during the 19th century and is now called plantation plainstyle.

The original house is hidden behind a two-story addition facing the road. This later section is decorated with a monumental two-story Greek Revival portico. Built entirely in wood, the portico has four square Doric columns supporting a pediment and a second-story wooden balcony.

The house was the center of a plantation which stretched to the nearby Savannah River and a village named Campbelltown. Established for commerce, Campbelltown had a ferry connection to Harrisburg across the Savannah. The small town disappeared after the establishment of Hamburg in the early 1820s

71. Green Meadows, *Richmond Hill Road and the Bobby Jones Expressway (about 1850).*

On a sandy ridge south of Augusta , this Greek Revival version of a plantation cottage, the single-story counterpart of plantation plain-style design, was built about 1850 with a commanding view of rolling rural land stretching northeast to the City of Augusta. the single story portico is a simple reference to the Greek Revival. The long floor-to-ceiling front windows are practical embellishments to this plantation house.

Today, the golf course of the Green Meadows Country Club and various layers of suburban South Augusta development cover the area between the former plantation and the City of Augusta limits. Generally, this area was transformed from rural to suburban after the completion of the Gordon Highway in 1957 and is known as South Augusta.

72. Thomas G. Lamar Plantation,
Old Aiken Road, Aiken County (about 1857).

Built on a South Carolina ridge approximately three miles north of the Savannah River on the road connecting Augusta and Aiken during the 19th century, the two-story house incorporates the spirit of the Greek Revival in its two-story portico. Without a pediment to support, the two-story square Doric columns demonstrate that even rustic versions of classical design can create a dramatic and imposing facade.

73. Butler House, *11 Butler Avenue,*
North Augusta, South Carolina (about 1857).

After its construction in the late 1850s, this Italianate villa was called the "Star of Edgefield."

The double veranda is decorated with cast iron, a material which first was made in Augusta in the late 1840s. Along with the third-story cupola, the porches originally provided a panoramic view of a hillside garden of paisley-shaped parterres and the city across the river. This garden is depicted in the North Augusta Land Company's town plan of 1891.

Brick construction and extensive use of cast iron were unusual for suburban villas built around Augusta during the 19th century. Instead of more commonplace frame construction, this house and the Goodale plantation are brick, probably made from nearby clay deposits. The introduction of steampowered machinery about 1850 led to the erection of new local brick factories capable of large-scale production.

In 1890, 5,000 acres of the Butler-Mealing land between this house and the river were purchased by North Augusta developers to develop the new suburban town.

74. Augusta National Golf Club ("Fruitland"),
2604 Washington Road, (about 1854).

When Dennis Redmond, editor of the agricultural newspaper *The Southern Cultivator* built this rustic villa as the center piece of his 250-acre nursery, "Fruitland", it was one of the first buildings in the South constructed with concrete walls. The design is based on a wraparound veranda raised over a high basement and enclosed by a high-pitched hipped roof (like ones used for many antebellum Louisiana plantation houses) capped with a central cupola. A description of the plantation house in an 1857 edition of *The Southern Cultivator* states that the house fulfills "the most obvious requirements of a Southern country house...ample space, shade, and ventilation."

In 1856, Prosper Jules Berckmans, a Belgian horticulturist, purchased the nursery land and, with his sons, made it one of the largest in the South. Fruitland Nursery was an expression of a widespread interest in horticulture and suburban landscaping which swept the United States beginning in the 1850s. The nursery business planned and planted local gardens, rows of street trees, and cultivated acres of shrubs and trees for national distribution.

In the early 1930s, the recently-founded Augusta National Golf Club bought the property and remodeled the interior of the house. United States Open golf champion (1930) Bobby Jones and Alastair McKenzie of Scotland designed a new golf course on the rolling grounds of the nursery, and the club started its annual sponsorship of the spring Masters tournament in 1934.

Through television coverage of the event played in a setting of tall pines, blooming azaleas, and dogwoods, the Augusta National club-house has become one of Augusta's most universally recognized sites.

The golf clubhouse stands at the end of a magnolia-lined lane leading from the commercial strip development along Washington Road. Beyond the club buildings and parking lots, the golf course sits on rolling land which gradually falls to the banks of Rae's Creek.

75. "Redcliffe" Plantation,
Beech Island, South Carolina (about 1859).

This Italianate plantation house shows how the universal building style introduced to Augusta in the 1850s was used in city, suburban, and rural areas. The front facade was originally designed with a single-story portico extending between the two second floor windows. The present wraparound veranda was added in the late 19th century.

Located on a 400-acre site approximately five miles east of Augusta on a South Carolina ridge, the plantation was devoted to ornamental trees, an orchard, an experimental vineyard supervised by an imported French vintner, and a variety of row crops. The house was built for South Carolina governor and United States Senator James H. Hammond and is attributed to prolific Augusta builder William H. Goodrich. "Redcliffe" is a larger but less detailed version of "Gould's Corner" in Summerville, which is also attributed to Goodrich.

The house is still located in its rural, Beech Island setting at the end of a magnolia allee. The design of the surrounding land is divided into two parts: north of the entrance drive is the functional landscape of row crops; south of the drive is a landscape of lawn and trees giving the effect of an 18th century English country house.

"Redcliffe" is operated as a house museum and reception center by the South Carolina Parks and Recreation Department.

76. Thurmond (Clarks Hill) Dam and Lake, *(1946-1952)*.

The $45 million, 5,860 foot long dam twenty-one miles northwest of Augusta was built by the U.S. Army Corps of Engineers to protect Augusta from floods, to increase river traffic, and to generate electricity. By spanning sections of both the Savannah River and the Little River, the dam created a 78,500-acre lake.

This federal building project has inspired a variety of residential and recreational building along its banks since its construction.

77. Fort Gordon and the Gordon Highway
(1940s through present).

Established in 1941 as Camp Gordon, the 56,000-acre home of the U.S. Army Signal Corps is located in southern Richmond County. After periods of high troop activity during World War II and the Korean War, the camp became a permanent army base in 1956.

The Gordon Highway was built from downtown Augusta to the military base during the early 1950s. The development of the elevated, section beginning at the Savannah River caused the demolition of historic houses between Elbert (Fourth) and center (Fifth) Streets.

78. Modern Industry:
a. Proctor & Gamble, *1962.*
b. Arcadian Corporation (Columbia Nitrogen), *1963.*
c. International Paper
(Federal Paperboard; Continental Can), *1963.*

The 1960s was a decade of new industrial growth by private corporations in southern and eastern Richmond County. All located on rural sites, these three factories are the largest in Richmond county. They were built on the edge of local suburban development in order to take advantage of low land costs.

International Paper

Arcardian Corporation

Proctor & Gamble

79. The Savannah River Site, *South Carolina (1951-1956)*

During the Cold War nuclear buildup of the 1950s, the United States government built one of the largest industrial facilities in the world at the time. In November 1950, the Atomic Energy Commission bought 315 square miles of rural land (including several small towns) fourteen miles southeast of Augusta in South Carolina. During the peak year of construction, 1952, 38,500 employees made their homes in the Aiken-Augusta area. Five nuclear reactors were eventually built.

As with Clarks Hill Dam and Fort Gordon, the scale of the project is linked to the goals and resources of the federal government. Although the industrial reservation is vast and has limited public access, its size and source of local jobs give it an undeniable presence as an Augusta landmark.

Index

Building/Site	Site #	Page